John

John

Annie Baker

THEATRE COMMUNICATIONS GROUP
NEW YORK
2016

John is published by Theatre Communications Group, Inc.,
520 Eighth Avenue, 24th Floor, New York, NY 10018-4156

Heinrich von Kleist (1777–1811), "On the Marionette Theatre," *Essays on Dolls*, Idris Parry, translator, Penguin, New York, 1994. "Gone," Smokey Rogers, songwriter, copyright © 1952; BMI/Hal Leonard Licensing. "I Want You," words and music by Bob Dylan, copyright © 1966, 1994 Dwarf Music; International Copyright Secured; All Rights Reserved; Reprinted by Permission. H. P. Lovecraft (1890–1937), "The Call of Cthulhu," copyright © 1926, *The Call of Cthulhu and Other Weird Stories*, Penguin, New York, 1999.

The publication of *John* by Annie Baker, through TCG's Book Program, is made possible in part by the New York State Council on the Arts with the support of Governor Andrew Cuomo and the New York State Legislature.

Special thanks to Paula Marie Black for her generous support of this publication.

TCG books are exclusively distributed to the book trade by Consortium Book Sales and Distribution.

LIBRARY OF CONGRESS CATALOGING-IN-PUBLICATION DATA
Baker, Annie, 1981–
John / Annie Baker.
ISBN 978-1-55936-529-1 (softcover)
ISBN 978-1-55936-528-4 (hardcover)
1. Marital conflict—Drama. 2. Interpersonal relations—Drama. 3. American. Family and Relationships. Marriage. Psychology. Interpersonal Relations.
PS3602.A5842 J64   2016
812'.6–dc23   2016008287|

Book design and composition by Lisa Govan
Cover image: Jean-Etienne Liotard, Marie-Anne Fancoise Liotard with a Doll, c.1774 Vienna Shonbrunn Palace

First Edition, May 2016
Second Printing, April 2017

The last page of this play is dedicated to Nico

———————

"Now, my excellent friend," said my companion, "you are in possession of all you need to know to follow my argument. We see that in the organic world, as thought grows dimmer and weaker, grace emerges more brilliantly and decisively. But just as a section drawn through two lines suddenly reappears on the other side after passing through infinity, or as the image in a concave mirror turns up again right in front of us after dwindling into the distance, so grace itself returns when knowledge has as it were gone through an infinity. Grace appears most purely in that human form which either has no consciousness or an infinite consciousness. That is, in the puppet or in the god."

—Heinrich von Kleist,
"On the Marionette Theatre"

John

Production History

John received its Off-Broadway world premiere at The Pershing Square Signature Center (James Houghton, Founding Artistic Director; Erika Mallin, Executive Director) in New York City, on August 8, 2015. It was directed by Sam Gold. The scenic design was by Mimi Lien, the costume design was by Ásta Bennie Hostetter, the lighting design was by Mark Barton, the sound design was by Bray Poor; the production stage manager was Amanda Michaels. The cast was:

ELIAS SCHREIBER-HOFFMAN	Christopher Abbott
JENNY CHUNG	Hong Chau
MERTIS KATHERINE GRAVEN	Georgia Engel
GENEVIEVE MARDUK	Lois Smith

SETTING

The first floor of a bed-and-breakfast in Gettysburg, Pennsylvania.

The very end of November.

There is a day porch and a little nook right off the day porch with a nonworking gas fireplace and leather armchair and a bookshelf, and then a much bigger room that is divided into two areas: a parlor area with a flowered couch and big stuffed armchairs and a magazine stand and lamps and a little tea rack and candy cupboard, and then a dining area with five or six round tables. The dining area has a Parisian theme, aka pictures of the Eiffel Tower and Eiffel Tower lamps and tablecloths with little berets or mimes on them.

The parlor area is full of small objects. There are gnomes and trolls on the shelves and glass menageries everywhere and tiny little porcelain angels playing the harp and tiny hand-sewn sayings in frames. There is an entire miniature wintertime railway and village. Maybe a birdcage with a little fake bird in it. There is a very large Christmas tree, probably not real, covered in white lights. There is a player piano and a ticking grandfather clock. Somewhere, hidden, there is a set of Swedish angel chimes. There is a CD player that is designed to look like a little jukebox from the '50s. It is always on and it is always playing Bach, softly.

There are two French doors upstage and their windows are covered by curtains. These doors lead to Mertis's wing of the house.

Then there's a big staircase leading from the parlor to the second floor and there's a landing and on the landing rests a terrifying American Girl doll in a doll-sized rocking chair.

Important

- Mertis opens and closes an old-school red velvet curtain between every act.

- During every scene transition Mertis sets the hands of the grandfather clock to the time of the following scene and changes the music on the jukebox. If she isn't the last person onstage, she stealthily creeps onstage between scenes to move time forward.

- " / " Indicates where the next line of dialogue begins.

Act One

Scene One

The house is empty. Nighttime. The jukebox radio is on. It is softly playing Bach's St. Matthew Passion, Aria No. 20.

Car lights swing across the room. The sound of an engine turning off. Car doors slam in the driveway. The doorbell rings. Ten seconds later, Mertis shuffles down the stairs onto the landing, then shuffles down the second flight of stairs into the parlor. She opens the door and goes out onto the day porch. We hear this:

MERTIS
(opening the door to the porch)
Hello!

ELIAS	JENNY
Hi! Hello!	Hi! So nice to . . .

She fades out. The sound of bags thumping up steps and across a threshold, knocking something aside.
Referring to something we don't see:

MERTIS	ELIAS
Oh my.	
It's fine.	Whoops, sorry.
Come on in!	
Get warm!	

Mertis holds the door open. Elias and Jenny enter, in big winter coats and maybe hats, dragging duffel bags. They look around.

JENNY	ELIAS
Wow.	
This is great.	Yeah.

MERTIS

Your home away from home.

JENNY

. . . So lovely!

MERTIS

Thank you.

She smiles at them and they wait for her to show them to their room.

MERTIS

Oh! I almost forgot!

She exits behind the French doors. Elias and Jenny look at each other. They smile.
Elias mouths: SHE'S A TRIP.

JENNY

What?

He mouths SHE'S A TRIP again.

JENNY

What?

Mertis reenters with a plate.

MERTIS

Peanut butter fudge.

JENNY   ELIAS
Oh wow.   That's so nice of you.

Mertis holds out the plate. They are still wearing coats and gloves and Elias is holding onto his duffel bag. Jenny takes off her gloves. Elias puts down his bag. He takes off his gloves. They both reach out and take a piece. They stand there awkwardly and take a bite while Mertis watches them.

ELIAS

That. Is. Good.

JENNY

Delicious.

Mertis watches them, beaming.

ELIAS

(his mouth full)
I'm Elias, by the way.

MERTIS

You were the one I spoke to on the phone!

ELIAS

Yup. And this is Jenny.

MERTIS

Hello Jenny.

9

JENNY

Hi.

ELIAS

And should we call / you—

MERTIS

Well I know it says Mertis on the website and Mertis Katherine is my proper name but most people just call me Kitty.

Elias swallows the last of his fudge. Jenny discreetly lowers the rest of her piece of fudge to her side. Elias picks up his bag.

MERTIS

I bet you'd like to see your room and get settled in.

JENNY   ELIAS
Great.   Yeah.

Mertis starts walking, then stops.

MERTIS

You'll have to excuse my slippers.

JENNY   ELIAS
Of course!   You're excused!

MERTIS

I have a blister and it's very late / so I was—

ELIAS

I'm sorry. I know we said nine. But there was crazy / traffic and—

MERTIS

It's fine, you're just not seeing me at my most glamorous.

They all walk toward the stairs. Mertis gestures toward the dining area.

MERTIS

Breakfast is from seven to nine.
We call this "Paris."

They gaze at Paris.

MERTIS

See. It's / got—

JENNY

Oh yeah!

MERTIS

You can come here for tea or hot cocoa. Any time of the day or night. Like a Paris café.

JENNY

Awesome.

ELIAS
(referring to a picture on the wall)
Who's that?

MERTIS

That's Eugenia.

Mertis continues toward a little nook with a mini-fridge and shelf full of snacks in the dining area.

MERTIS

There's Pepsi and seltzer water.
Please help yourself to whatever you like.
   (she opens the mini-fridge door, closes it, then points to the shelf)
And candy and cookies up there.

JENNY

Dangerous.

MERTIS

Well.

It can be, yes.

It can be very dangerous. But I think of it for guests only.

I'm on a very strict diet.

(stage whisper)

Sixty-seven pounds in four months.

JENNY   ELIAS

That's amazing.   Wow. / Wait—

MERTIS

It's the HCG diet . . . have you heard of HCG?

They shake their heads no.

MERTIS

You give yourself these special injections and you cut out all refined sugar.

They don't know what to say to this.

MERTIS

There's a wonderful doctor who wrote a book about it. I'll show you tomorrow.

Mertis finally heads up the stairs. They follow. Jenny stops on the landing to stare at the doll. Then follows Mertis and Elias.
On the second set of stairs:

MERTIS

(pointing up to an object we can't see)

Now that is genuine Civil War era!

ELIAS

Cool.

MERTIS
(out of sight now, in the upstairs hallway)
... And ... let's see ... you're in the Chamberlain room ...

ELIAS
(hesitating on the stairs)
I thought we were in the Jackson.

MERTIS

Oh—really? Because the Jackson—I think the Chamberlain is much nicer.

ELIAS

I think we asked for the Jackson though.

Pause.

MERTIS

Yes well I'm going to be honest with you the Jackson has a leak. A leak in the ceiling.

JENNY

Oh.

MERTIS

You probably asked for the Jackson because it's the least expensive but I'm going to give you the Chamberlain for the price of the Jackson and I hope you'll forgive me for not giving you ample warning.

JENNY   ELIAS
Well thanks for the deal!   No, it's okay.

They head up the stairs and disappear into the upstairs hallway. Footsteps. The sound of a door unlocking. This next section is heard faintly. We shouldn't catch all of it.

MERTIS

Who's tall enough to reach the dolphin? That string with the dolphin.

More footsteps.

MERTIS

Well. All right. This is my favorite room in the house.

JENNY

I really like the ceiling.

MERTIS

That's what they call a memory wheel!

Pause. Sound of bags being set down on the floor.

MERTIS

Let's see. We have oil heat and the upstairs gets terribly hot if it stays on at night so I turn it off at nine P.M. But some guests like to be toasty while they're sleeping so there's a little space heater in the closet if you need it.

More footsteps.

JENNY

Thank you, Mertis.
Kitty.

MERTIS

I—what time do you think you'll be coming down for breakfast? Closer to seven or closer to nine?

JENNY
Uh—

ELIAS
Hmm—

MERTIS

I just like to have some sense.

ELIAS

. . . Probably closer to nine.

MERTIS

Mmhm. All right. Young people usually come down closer to
nine.
   (exiting the room)
I hope you have a nice sleep and that you . . . that you enjoy
yourselves.

JENNY   ELIAS
Good night.   Thanks! Good night!

*Sound of the bedroom door shutting. Sound of Mertis walking down
the hallway and down the stairs. She steps carefully down to the
landing. She continues down the stairs. She walks slowly across the
room, switching off all the lamps except one. She does this methodi-
cally, with care. As she switches off the last one, she hears some of the
following faintly from upstairs and pauses:*

ELIAS   JENNY
   (offstage)   *(offstage, faintly)*
No. No. You have no idea
how—
I should have the right to
say whatever I—   Yes but—
Because that's how I feel. But you said it in this way
Isn't that what you want?   that—
I'M TELLING YOU HOW
I FEEL.   Okay, okay. Stop yelling.
I'm not yelling.

*Mertis waits, her hand on the lamp switch, and then turns it off. She
makes her way across the room. She stops at the little jukebox. She
changes the music to Bach's Passacaglia for Organ in C Minor. She
changes the hands on the clock to 2:04. The moon rises. She walks to
her little curtained set of French doors. She disappears behind them.*

Scene Two

It is 2:04 A.M. The jukebox is still playing the Passacaglia for Organ in C Minor.

Jenny walks down the stairs, sock-footed, wrapped in a quilt covered in pictures of little girls in bonnets.

She thinks for a moment, then walks back up the stairs.

Faint sounds of a door creaking open, then a door closing a few seconds later.

Jenny comes back down the stairs, lugging a space heater. She lugs it down to the parlor and starts looking around for outlets. She finds an outlet not that near the couch. She looks for another one for a while, in vain. Then she settles on the one that's not that near the couch. She plugs it in, then drags the space heater as close as she can to the couch.

It starts humming and blowing. She presses a button and puts it on the setting that makes it turn its little head in circles around the room. She lies down on the couch and tries to get as much of her body as possible under the quilt.

*She changes her mind about the space heater, gets up, and changes
the setting so it just blows air toward the couch.*
She turns down the music.
She notices an object that is out of place or toppled over. She rights it.
*She sits back down and stares at the doll sitting on the landing in
the rocking chair.*
A door creaks open upstairs. Footsteps.
Elias appears on the landing in his boxers and a T-shirt.
They regard each other.

ELIAS

What is happening.

JENNY

I'm so cold and I also feel like I'm about to get my period.

A long pause.

JENNY

See that doll?

ELIAS

What doll?

JENNY

There.

Elias turns and looks at the American Girl doll in the rocking chair.

JENNY

That's Samantha.

He doesn't get it.

JENNY

She's the one I had when I was a kid.

ELIAS

The scary one?

Jenny nods.

ELIAS

It's the same doll?

JENNY

Yup.

They both look at Samantha.

JENNY

Doesn't she look mad?

Elias leans down and peers at her face.

ELIAS

Not really.

He picks up Samantha and turns her upside down to inspect her crotch.

JENNY

What are you doing?
Stop it!

ELIAS

She's wearing white cotton underwear.

He starts to touch the underwear.

JENNY

Don't look underneath it!
She'll never forgive you!

> ELIAS

Are you serious?

> JENNY

Please don't.

> ELIAS

Okay, okay.

He puts Samantha back in her rocking chair and smooths her hair.

> JENNY

It's really freaking me out.
It's the same outfit and everything.
I feel like she found me.

> ELIAS

Where is your Samantha?

> JENNY

In Columbus.
In the basement.

> ELIAS

Do you think she's pissed that you put her in a basement?

> JENNY

I can't even—I can't even think about it.

Pause.

> ELIAS

I gotta go back to sleep.

Elias walks back upstairs. The door to the Chamberlain room creaks shut.
Jenny sits there. Then she stands up, still wrapped in the quilt, and starts to walk toward the staircase. Then she changes her mind. She

walks over to the piano. She puts a finger on it. The piano starts playing "Yes Sir, That's My Baby." Jenny jumps back in terror. The piano keeps playing itself. It looks like a ghost is playing it. Eventually Elias comes back down the stairs onto the landing. They silently watch the ghost play the piano. The song ends. The space heater is still blowing. Jenny looks up at Elias. Elias looks down at Jenny from the landing.

JENNY

I didn't do that on purpose.

Pause.

JENNY

Come sit next to me.
Just for a minute.

Pause.

JENNY

I'll rub your neck.

A pause. Then Elias slowly walks down the stairs and joins her on the couch. A negotiation involving the blanket. Then Jenny starts giving Elias a neck rub with one hand. He gazes around the room.

ELIAS

There's so much miniature shit.
Are you super into it?

JENNY

It's actually too much.
I can't look at it.

ELIAS

It's like a Jenny Chung wet dream.

JENNY

I start grinding my teeth.
When there's too much small stuff I get so excited that I grind
my teeth.

She takes her hand off his neck for a second to touch her jawbone.

JENNY

And I left my stupid mouth guard in Columbus.

ELIAS

Tell them to mail it.

JENNY

I did.

Pause.

ELIAS

Is it the railroad? Did that make you grind your teeth?

JENNY

No.
It's the town hall and the tiny people having like a tiny mayoral
meeting around a tiny table if you peep through the window.

ELIAS

Where.

She points without looking. He looks.

ELIAS

Oh.
Yeah.

Pause. They sit there. She rubs his neck.

21

JENNY

Tell me a story.

ELIAS

Happy or sad?

JENNY

Scary.
Tell me a scary story.

ELIAS

I don't know if I can like make up a scary story on the spot.

JENNY

Try.

ELIAS

Do you think it's scary here?

JENNY

A little.

ELIAS

Yeah.
But more tragic than scary.

JENNY

Why tragic?

ELIAS

You know. The tchotchkes.
"Paris."
The like Tragedy of Bed-and-Breakfasts.
The like desperate attempts to be homey and special and cheer-
ful and warm and cute.
I don't know.
Isn't it obvious?

JENNY

Do you think my parents' house is tragic?

ELIAS

Jenny.

JENNY

Because my mother has a lot of cheerful tchotchkes.

ELIAS

Your parents' house is . . .

Pause.

ELIAS

I feel trapped.

JENNY

I'm just asking.

ELIAS

But I'm actually getting really anxious because I feel you trapping me.

JENNY

There's not like a wrong answer to my question. So I don't / see—

ELIAS

PLEASE STOP TRAPPING / ME.

JENNY

Okay please don't yell.

They sit in silence. Her hand is frozen still on the back of his neck.

ELIAS

Can you take your hand off my neck?

She slowly removes her hand from his neck.

                                    JENNY
I don't know why that turned into a fight.

                                    ELIAS
That wasn't a fight.

He collapses back and closes his eyes. He breathes. After a while:

                                    ELIAS
It was a
Cold
Dark
Rainy Night.
A man and a woman were driving down a highway at night.
A highway in the American Midwest.
And then they realized . . .
They realized they were low on gas.
And they . . .
And they looked for a gas station but there weren't any and it
was pouring rain and they could barely see through the wind-
shield so they pulled into this, uh, creepy motel by the side of
the highway.
And they walked into the motel and there was an old man
with one eye.
Sitting at the, uh, front desk.

Pause.

                                    ELIAS
And the old man with one eye had them . . . he told them . . .
he had them sign their names in the . . . logbook . . . and
uh . . . he told them they could have any room they wanted in
the motel. Because it was totally empty. And so the man and
the woman picked a room and they uh . . . they brought their
bags up to the room and they got into bed and then . . .

And then they realized . . .
That there was a face at the window.
Watching them.
And it was the face of . . .

Pause.

ELIAS

I'm stuck.

JENNY

It's so good!

ELIAS

I can only do build-up to scary.
Not scary itself.

JENNY

That's okay.

ELIAS

You wanted scary.

JENNY

I just want you to keep going.

Pause.

ELIAS

And the face in the window was . . .

Pause.

ELIAS

I'm done.

He stands up.

JENNY

I'm still cold.

ELIAS

Good night Jenny.

Elias gets up and starts walking up the stairs. He stops on the landing.

ELIAS

I should have made it Gettysburg-specific.
Like "Ghosts of Gettysburg." All the dead soldiers and shit.
Spirits haunting the Devil's Den.

JENNY

I liked the face.

Elias shakes his head and heads upstairs.

Scene Three

Morning.
9:17 on the grandfather clock.
The first movement of the Brandenburg Concerto is playing on the jukebox.
Elias is sitting at a table in Paris pouring cereal from a little cereal box and then pouring milk from a little silver pitcher.
Jenny is standing nearby looking at the newspaper selection on a coffee table. She picks through it. She picks the front section and the Arts and Leisure section.
She walks back to the table and hands Elias the Arts and Leisure section. She sits at the table.
Elias starts looking at the front page of the folded Arts and Leisure section on the tabletop and eating his cereal.
His eating is too loud for her.
It is annoying her.
Eventually Jenny takes one hand off the front section of the newspaper and very very subtly puts a finger in her ear while still trying to prop the front section up. She turns a page. He looks up and notices.

ELIAS

What.

JENNY

What.

ELIAS

What's that?

JENNY

What.

ELIAS

That.

JENNY

Oh. Nothing.

She takes her finger out of her ear and turns another page of the newspaper.

ELIAS

Are / you like—

JENNY

It's nothing.

He goes back to eating. She goes back to reading. As he's eating it occurs to him what was happening.

ELIAS

Were you doing that because I was eating too loudly?

JENNY

No.

ELIAS

Because you can just tell me that I'm eating too loudly.

Pause.

ELIAS

You don't have to like passive-aggressively notify me through physical behavior. You can be honest with me. Remember?

Pause.

JENNY

Okay.

Elias gazes at her. Then he picks up his spoon and starts eating again. Jenny tries to bear it, but then can't help herself.

JENNY

Yes okay fine.

ELIAS

What.

JENNY

Sorry.
I guess it was a tiny bit too loud.

ELIAS

And that bothers you / because—

JENNY

It's just a little gross.

ELIAS

(calmly)
What's gross about it.

JENNY

It's like . . .
Whatever.
Sorry.

ELIAS

No tell me.

JENNY

It's just kind of a gross sound.
I can like hear you like breathing and smacking your tongue /
against the—

ELIAS

Sounds very Jewish.

JENNY

Wait, what?

ELIAS

Like, oh Jesus, the big loud hairy Jew is like smacking his
lips again and chewing with his mouth open and it's totally
repulsive.

JENNY

It has nothing to do with you being Jewish.

ELIAS

That's what you think.

JENNY

Oh my god.

Mertis wanders in through the French doors with a tray of food.

MERTIS

Here are the eggs . . .

She puts the eggs down.

MERTIS

And then I have a little—

She wanders off.
Elias and Jenny stare at the eggs.

ELIAS

These are not real eggs.

JENNY

Yes they are.

ELIAS

They're like fake . . . they're like mix.

JENNY

No I know what the mix ones look like.

ELIAS

They don't look like real eggs.

JENNY

That's because she used a—

Mertis comes back in with a plate with two lumpen brown cakey
things on it. She proudly places it on the table between them.

MERTIS

And this is homemade.
Homemade duff.

JENNY

Wow! Wait, what's it called?

MERTIS

Sailor's duff.

She wanders off again.
They look at the Sailor's duff.
They don't speak.
Mertis reenters.

31

MERTIS

It's a family recipe.
There's a very funny . . .
We would always make it on New Year's Day.
And the joke was . . .
You eat the duff,
And then ten minutes later you have thud.

Mertis is amused.

JENNY

I don't get it.

MERTIS

Oh no. I'm not explaining it properly.
You eat the duff, and the feeling . . . the feeling you get after
eating the duff . . . that's called thud.

She wanders off again.
They pick up their forks.

JENNY

Look, I know it's not mix because my mom would use a mix.
The reason this looks weird is because she has a little egg frying machine.
This is how they look when you pour them into a little egg frying machine and don't just use a normal pan.

ELIAS

It looks fake.

JENNY

It's not.
They're eggs.

Jenny begins to eat. She is angry and doesn't want to be angry.
After a while:

JENNY

I just want to say that what I was—that the chewing loudly has nothing to do with you being Jewish and that you / always—

ELIAS

But how would you know?

JENNY

How would I know?

ELIAS

How would you know if it was a Jewish thing?

JENNY

Because that's like a stereotype.

ELIAS

That might be based in a reality of a / cultural—

JENNY

So what are you saying? That Jews are like disgusting—

ELIAS

No I'm saying that there are certain cultural—I mean you of all people should / understand—

JENNY

What is that supposed / to—

ELIAS

You of all people should understand that there are weird cultural things and certain things are like—like the way you hate— how you hate when I point? When I'm making a—the way I point my finger at you?

JENNY

I don't like the way you get amped up and start pointing and waving your arms around.

ELIAS

Yeah but see that's a Jewish thing.

JENNY

No.
No.
I don't accept that.

ELIAS

You don't get to not accept it, you / can—

JENNY

It's not a Jewish thing, it's you being loud or domineering or you being gross, and you're making it a Jewish thing so I sound like I'm anti-Semitic or something.

ELIAS

I never said you were anti-Semitic.
I was trying to *let you in on my experience.*
I'm trying to tell you *that my whole family eats like this.*

JENNY

Um, okay Eli, but believe it or not I have spent time with other Jews besides you, and and and Deena, and Lexie, and Adam, and it's not a—they don't like slurp their cereal like you do. They eat like normal people.

Pause.

ELIAS

Wow.
Normal people.

Another pause.

ELIAS

Well then you're just dating a particularly repulsive person.
A like abnormally disgusting guy.

I mean, what a terrible thing to be in.
To be with someone you find repulsive.
I can see how that would make you—

Mertis wanders in again.

JENNY

(quietly)
You know that's not the issue.

Mertis sits at the table next to them.
They smile at her. She smiles back.

MERTIS

I don't know why it's called Sailor's duff but that's what we
always called it.

Pause.

MERTIS

How are the eggs?

ELIAS   JENNY
Great.   Really great.

MERTIS

What are your plans for today?

They look at each other.

JENNY   ELIAS
Elias wants to—   We were just gonna do the
                                         auto tour.
                                         With the CD from the visitor's
                                         center.

35

MERTIS

Oh the one with Percy Nesbitt!

ELIAS

Is that the one they sell at the visitor's center?

MERTIS

That's the official—everyone loves that one.

JENNY

Oh good.

MERTIS

Where are you having dinner?

ELIAS

We were just gonna drive around and look / for a—

MERTIS

Have you heard about the Dobbin House?

They shake their heads no.

MERTIS

It's the oldest house in town and there's a very good historical-type dinner and they're in the old-fashioned getup and the menu has the strangest things on it . . . like a peanut soup! Apparently everyone ate peanut soup back then—and you sit in this very old room and there are these very strange paintings on the wall and then *upstairs* there's a sort of . . . a diorama and you stand in this room and you look up . . . and in the floorboards there's a sort of slave diorama!

Pause.

ELIAS

What's a slave diorama?

MERTIS

There are these life-sized uh . . . slaves and they're hiding in the floorboards and it's a very realistic reenactment of the Underground Railroad.

ELIAS

Wait, they're real people? Real people are playing the slaves?

MERTIS

No. No. They're mummies.

They look at her.

MERTIS

Not mummies. Manni—mun—

JENNY

Mannequins?

MERTIS

Yes. These very realistic mannequins and you can see how the slaves hid in the floorboards before they headed north to freedom!

Her phone rings. It's attached to a little fanny pack she wears around her waist. She looks at it.

MERTIS

I'm so sorry. I don't usually . . . but it's my friend Genevieve and she's a bit older and she's also blind and I / make a point of—

JENNY

Please get it!
Please don't worry about it!

Mertis answers the phone.

MERTIS

Genevieve?
Yes.
I can't understand you.
I'm with some guests.

Jenny gestures no-no-please!

MERTIS

(into the phone)
It was John Henry Newman!

She moves slowly toward the French doors.

MERTIS

(into the phone)
"Numquam minus solus quam cum solus."

She disappears behind the doors.
A pause.

JENNY

Do you think anyone else is staying here?

Elias doesn't respond.

JENNY

You know I don't think you're repulsive.

Pause.

JENNY

I think you're so beautiful.
I think you're the most beautiful person I've ever met.

A painful pause while she waits for him to say that she's beautiful too. He takes a bite of eggs, then:

ELIAS

(mouth full)
See, now I'm self-conscious / about how I—

JENNY

Do you think I'm beautiful?

ELIAS

Sure.

She reaches out and touches his wrist. They look at each other sadly.

JENNY

Hold on.

Jenny gets up and hurries upstairs. Her iPhone is sitting on the breakfast table, face down. Elias is alone. He eats cereal. He eats enthusiastically, then decides to try eating quietly. It's hard. How do people do it? Jenny's phone dings. She has received a text. Elias stares at her phone. Then he glances up at the staircase. He is about to reach forward to pick up the phone when Mertis opens the French doors and pokes her head out. He withdraws his hand.

MERTIS

I forgot to ask.
Was everything all right in the Chamberlain room last night?

ELIAS

Uh. Yeah. Great.

MERTIS

Because I thought I heard / someone—

ELIAS

Well. Jenny was a little cold so she ended up sleeping down here until the heat came back on upstairs.

MERTIS

Oh dear.

ELIAS

She's always cold, though.
Her fingers and toes are like these ice blocks.

MERTIS

Did she try using the space heater?

ELIAS

It wasn't enough.

MERTIS

I apologize. I'll turn it up tonight.

ELIAS

That would be great.

MERTIS

I have to warn you. It gets pretty steamy.

ELIAS

She'll love that.

She smiles at him and ducks back into her quarters. The door shuts behind her. Jenny slides on her butt down a few steps toward the landing. Elias is in the middle of gazing at her phone again when Jenny hisses:

JENNY

Psssst.

ELIAS

Whoa. What?
Why are you sitting?

JENNY

I just got my period.

ELIAS

Fuck.

JENNY

It's bad.
It's gonna be really really bad.

ELIAS

Did you take ibuprofen?

JENNY

Five.

ELIAS

You took five?!

JENNY

Just now.

ELIAS

That's too much.

Pause.

JENNY

I'm not sure I can go out today.

ELIAS

Jenny.

JENNY

I'm dying.
I feel like I'm giving birth.

ELIAS

We'll just do the auto tour. You can stay in the car the whole time.

JENNY

I actually feel like I'm giving birth to my own uterus.

ELIAS

Let's wait for the ibuprofen to kick in and then we'll see how you feel.

Pause.

ELIAS

This is really important to me.

JENNY

Okay.

She starts to crawl back upstairs.

ELIAS

Where are you going?

JENNY

To lie down until the ibuprofen kicks in.
Is that my phone?

ELIAS

What?

JENNY

Is that my phone on the table?

ELIAS

Oh. I guess so.

JENNY

Will you bring it to me?

He brings the phone to her. She takes it and crawls back upstairs out of view. Elias is alone for a while. He walks over to the small oil painting of Eugenia on the wall and peers closely at it. There is something about it that's troubling him. Mertis reenters. She stands there. Then:

MERTIS

There was a reason I came out again.
I wanted to tell you something.

Pause.

MERTIS

I'll be dipped.

ELIAS

That's okay.
You can / just—

MERTIS

Oh yes!
You wanted to know about HCG.

She leaves and then reenters again carrying a book and a jar of black liquid.
She hands the book to Elias.
He holds it, puzzled.

MERTIS

It's a pregnancy hormone.
You give yourself daily injections and you don't eat more than seven hundred calories a day.

ELIAS

That sounds really intense.

                              MERTIS

Read the back!
He's a doctor.

Elias turns the book over and reads the back.

                              ELIAS

Huh.

                              MERTIS

Two meals a day.
I skip breakfast.
Every meal has to include one protein one vegetable one bread
and one fruit.
No butters or oils.
And you drink this every morning.

*She holds up the jar, which is pitch-black and maybe flecked with
tiny pieces of gold or silver.*

                              ELIAS

What is that?

                              MERTIS

It's this special potion.
It's 12 on the pH scale so it's very alka—alkalinizing and
apparently it has lots of vitamin K and B and a very powerful
live probiotic.
They send you the packets in the mail.

                              ELIAS

Why is it black?

                              MERTIS

    (gazing at it)
I don't know.

ELIAS

(flipping through the book)
Are you supposed to lose that much weight that fast?
Isn't that supposed / to be—

MERTIS

I've never felt better in my life.
No alcohol.
No refined sugar.

He hands the book back to her. He looks at the potion.

ELIAS

What does it taste like?

Mertis holds out the jar. Elias hesitates, then takes a sip.

ELIAS

. . . Huh.
Weird.
What's that flavor?
It's kind of familiar but I can't place it.

MERTIS

Not bad, right?

ELIAS

Rain on concrete?
Bananas?

Pause.

MERTIS

Have a wonderful day, Elias.

ELIAS

Yeah.
Thanks, Mertis. You too.

MERTIS

You can also call me Kitty.

ELIAS

Right.
Kitty.

Mertis turns around and walks back through the French doors.

Scene Four

Late afternoon. 4:48 on the clock. The sun is starting to set. No music.
Mertis is sitting in a window seat or in a chair by the window in
the parlor area, scribbling in a dusty notebook.
The sound of a car door slamming, then driving away.
Jenny enters, bundled up. She walks into the parlor, hoping no one
is there. Her face falls when she sees Mertis.

MERTIS

How was the tour?!

JENNY

It was okay. I didn't finish it. I'm not feeling so good.

MERTIS

Can I get you some / tea or some—

JENNY

I'm just gonna go upstairs and lie down.

MERTIS

All right.

Jenny trudges up the first flight of stairs. She stops and looks at Samantha. Then she turns around.

JENNY

Sorry, how was your day?

MERTIS

It was lovely! I bought some groceries and ran into a couple of friends and then George and I ate lunch together.

JENNY

Who's George?

MERTIS

My husband.

JENNY

Oh!
Okay.

Pause.

JENNY

. . . Does George live here?

MERTIS

Of course!

JENNY

Just . . . um . . .

Jenny gestures toward the French doors.

MERTIS

Yes, yes, of course!

JENNY

Oh wow.
I didn't realize that.

MERTIS

Are you sure I can't make you some tea?

JENNY

I'm fine. Thank you.

Jenny exits upstairs.
Mertis goes over to the jukebox radio and turns it on. Bach's
Cantata No 82 comes piping in. She goes back to scribbling by the
window.
Jenny reappears at the top of the stairs.

JENNY

Sorry.
Um. Sorry.
But um . . .
The Chamberlain room is still really cold.

MERTIS

It is?!

JENNY

Yes.

MERTIS

Wait one minute.
Let me go turn on the heat.

Mertis walks across the room and through the French doors.

A few seconds later, she walks back in.

JENNY

I'm sorry. Um. Wait. So, the heat wasn't on at all upstairs?

> MERTIS

Well it gets really steamy up there.

> JENNY

Uh-huh.

> MERTIS

So when the guests are gone during the day I turn it off.

Pause.

> MERTIS

I didn't think you'd be coming back till later.

> JENNY

But didn't you say that you also turn it off at night?

Pause.

> MERTIS

I'll leave it on.
I apologize.

Pause.

> MERTIS

It's nice and toasty down here.
Why don't you join me?

Pause.

> JENNY

Let me just take some ibuprofen.

Jenny leaves. A few seconds later she reappears, sweatered and sock-footed, and schlumps down the staircase and onto the couch. She takes out her iPhone and rests it on her chest. She lies there.

MERTIS

Where's Elias?

JENNY

He's finishing the battlefield tour. And then going to dinner.

Pause.

JENNY

I have really bad cramps. I just couldn't do it anymore. I sat in
that car for five hours.
And the painkillers make me feel like I'm gonna throw up.
Sorry if I'm being rude.

MERTIS

No, no. It's a terrible thing.

Pause.

MERTIS

Did you learn anything exciting today?

JENNY

Well. I mean. I don't really know anything about Gettysburg.
So we did . . . uh . . . Seminary Ridge . . . and Devil's Den . . .
and the Peach Orchard . . . that was kind of creepy . . .

MERTIS

Mmhm . . .

JENNY

And then I pooped out and made him drive me home.
Oh, and we did the uh . . . Little Round Top. Where Chamberlain saved the day. And I was like: oh yeah—our room was
named after him!

MERTIS

What brought you to Gettysburg?

51

JENNY

Well, when Elias was a kid he was totally obsessed with the Civil War. It's funny, cuz he was raised by hippies in California but like . . . yeah. When he was nine he wanted to be a Civil War historian. Not a musician.

MERTIS

He's a musician?

JENNY

Yeah. He's a drummer.
Slash computer programmer.
Anyway, when we knew we were gonna be driving back from Ohio he got really excited about taking a detour and spending a couple of nights here. He's been rereading all his old books.
(after a short pause)
You must be like a Gettysburg expert.

MERTIS

Oh no. I've never even been on a tour!

JENNY

Really?

MERTIS

Once I drove through part of the battlefield on my way to Wegmans. But I didn't know what anything was or what anything meant. I just liked looking at those old fences.

JENNY

Huh.
I guess that's like . . .
I live in Brooklyn and I've never been to Ellis Island.

Pause. Jenny writes a text. While typing, absentmindedly:

JENNY

Did you grow up around here?

MERTIS

No, I grew up all over.

My sister used to work at Hanover Hospital and when I was going through a difficult time about fifteen years ago she encouraged me to move here and take a job at the hospital with her. So I did.

JENNY

Were you a nurse?

MERTIS

Oh no. My sister was a nurse. I just cleaned bedpans.

JENNY

Oh. Okay.

MERTIS

A year or two ago I ran into one of the doctors. And he wasn't always the nicest man when I worked there. I'm sure he was very busy and had a lot on his mind, but I think he wasn't as kind to me as he could have been. Anyway, he recognized me and he said: "What are you up to now, Mertis?" And I said: "Well, sir, I'm running a B&B with my husband and I'm doing quite well."

And that was a nice little moment in my life.

JENNY

Yeah! Screw that guy.

A weird pause. Mertis contemplates saying something, but then goes back to her notebook.

JENNY

Is that a journal?

MERTIS

Sort of.

I just use it to describe things.

Nothing too personal.

Right now I'm trying to describe the sunset.

Jenny cranes her neck to gaze out the window.

JENNY

What are you saying about it?

Mertis reads from her notebook:

MERTIS

"The white November sky morphed into an exquisite robin's egg blue by 4 P.M., and its welcome presence lasted but a short while. By 4:45, phosphorescent oranges, grotesque reds, and blasphemous purples slashed open the sky, followed by a slow and oozing transformation into a brooding, subfuscous indigo, which now, as I write this, leads us inexorably down the ever-darkening path from the gloaming into night."

JENNY

. . . Wow.

MERTIS

I try to document it every day if I can.

A comfortable silence while Jenny plays with her iPhone and Mertis writes. Jenny's phone dings once or twice as she receives texts. Then:

MERTIS

What are you doing on that thing?

JENNY

Oh. Well. I'm actually working, if you can believe it. I'm researching something. And I'm also texting my sister.

MERTIS

What are you researching?

JENNY

I write questions for a game show.
(short pause)
Have you heard of Cash Cow?

MERTIS

Oh my goodness. Genevieve loves Cash Cow! I've never seen
it but she talks about it constantly!

JENNY

I write their questions. I mean, me and six other people.

MERTIS

What a fascinating job!

JENNY

It's okay.

MERTIS

You must be very smart!

JENNY

I mean, I don't have any kind of comprehensive knowledge.
I just have a lot of weird random factoids at my fingertips.

MERTIS

Ooh, tell me one.

JENNY

Well, I'm like contractually . . . I can't talk about any questions
that haven't aired on the show yet. Because then you could
like . . . you could like remember what I told you and then go
on the show and win like two million dollars and even if that
wasn't intentional cheating it actually would be like . . .

Um . . .

Hmmm.

I'm trying to think of one that already aired.

Mmm . . .

Oh!

What nation's flag has a white dragon in its center that is said to symbolize purity?

You get 100,000 dollars if you guess this one right.

(A) Brunei, (B) Bhutan, (C) Burkina Faso, or (D) Burundi.

MERTIS

. . . A white dragon?

JENNY

Said to symbolize purity.

Brunei, Bhutan, Burkina Faso, or Burundi.

Pause.

MERTIS

. . . Bhutan.

JENNY

Yes!

MERTIS

I'll be dipped.

JENNY

Wait, did you already know that?!

MERTIS

I just guessed.

JENNY

That's awesome.

MERTIS

I'm also a tiny bit of a mind reader.

She goes back to her notebook. Jenny is slightly weirded-out.

JENNY

I just thought of another one that already aired.

MERTIS

Shoot.

JENNY

The eye of an ostrich is (A) Half the size of its brain (B) The same size as its brain . . . um . . . (C) Twice as large as its brain, or (D) Three times as large as its brain?

MERTIS

(C) Twice as large.

JENNY

That's right!
That's crazy!
Did you just guess that one again?

MERTIS

No, no, I knew that answer.
I'm very fond of birds and I try to learn as much about them as possible.

JENNY

Don't tell Elias that. He has bird-phobia.

Jenny's phone rings.

MERTIS

Bird-phobia?

Mertis glances at a bird on the wall. Jenny answers the phone and wanders into Paris while she talks to Elias.

JENNY

Hi.

Yeah.

No I'm in uh . . .

I'm in Paris.

Yeah. Talking to Mertis.

   (pause)

Yes I'm still in pain.

What does that mean?

   (pause)

That's totally fine.

   (pause)

Yeah.

No it's fine.

Aren't those like huge . . .

Aren't they like scams?

   (pause)

Whatever. It's totally fine.

I'll text you if I'm feeling better.

Yup.

I'll order in or whatever.

I love—

He hangs up. Jenny looks at her phone despondently.

MERTIS

Was that Elias?

JENNY

He wants to go on one of those graveyard ghost tours.

Pause.

JENNY

With the like . . . with the night vision goggles.

Uch.
So dumb.

MERTIS

What are you going to do?

JENNY

I don't know. He has the car.
I guess I'll just stay here and fact-check and text my sister.

Silence for a while. Jenny texts; Mertis writes. Then Mertis looks up.

MERTIS

Would you like to meet Genevieve?

End of Act One
Intermission One

Act Two

Scene One

8:54 P.M.
Jenny, Genevieve and Mertis are all sitting around a table.
An open bottle of white wine.
All three women are holding wine glasses but Mertis is drinking water out of hers.
The irises of Genevieve's eyes are so pale blue they're nearly white. She is blind.
Genevieve is telling a story.
Jenny is a little tipsy.

GENEVIEVE

That was around the time I went crazy.

MERTIS

Oh Genevieve.

GENEVIEVE

It's true.
I was clinically insane!
That's what they called me!

JENNY

How were you—what / was the—

GENEVIEVE

I was convinced that my ex-husband had taken possession of
my soul and that his spirit was trying to destroy me.
    (stage whisper)
The thing about being crazy is it can also all be true.

*Mertis slowly gets to her feet and starts walking toward the French
doors.*

GENEVIEVE

I hear you walking away, Mertis!

MERTIS

I'm just getting us some Vienna Fingers.

Mertis is gone.

GENEVIEVE

I left him in '64. In '65 I woke up and I realized that he was
still with me. He was still inside my body. All his judgments
and his thoughts. I had left him but he hadn't left me!
I didn't get out of bed for a month. He wouldn't let me move.
I felt his fingers opening and closing my lids.
Now you sleep.
Now you wake.

Mertis reenters with a plate of Vienna Fingers.

GENEVIEVE

Sometimes I would have a thought of my own and he'd say:
THAT THOUGHT IS MY THOUGHT.
"THAT THOUGHT IS MY THOUGHT."

JENNY

Wait, he wasn't there? He / was—

GENEVIEVE

No no no no. I'd left him back in California.

MERTIS

Jenny, would you like a Vienna Finger?

JENNY

No thanks.

MERTIS

Genevieve?

GENEVIEVE

Yes please.

Mertis holds the plate out and Genevieve gropes for and then begins munching on a Vienna Finger. (She will consume at least five more before she leaves.)

JENNY

So then what happened?

GENEVIEVE

I checked myself into an institution.
Only to discover he had insinuated himself into the minds of all the doctors and nurses.
HE was prescribing me my medication.
HE was the psychiatrist assigned to my case.
Don't you see that you're imagining things? HE would say to me.

My roommate started to say things that only HE would say.
She began singing OUR song under her breath.
One time she started humming it in the middle of the night.
How do you know that song?!
What song?
That song!
The song you were just humming!
I wasn't humming anything.
I was fast asleep.

JENNY

What was the song?

GENEVIEVE

(in a warbling voice)
Since you're gone
The stars, the moon
The sun in the sky
Know the reason why I cry

Mertis joins in singing.

GENEVIEVE AND MERTIS

Love Divine
Once was mine
Now you're gone . . .

GENEVIEVE

Mertis knows it.

MERTIS

That song was sung by the great Ferlin Husky.

GENEVIEVE

Now I could use this as proof that HE is still invading the thoughts and memories of those close to me. Including my dearest friend Mertis Katherine.
I am choosing to believe otherwise.

JENNY

What was his name?

GENEVIEVE

John.
But I called him Jack.

JENNY

Oh. That's funny.

GENEVIEVE

Why?

JENNY

I just . . . I just know someone named John.

GENEVIEVE

Everyone knows someone named John.

MERTIS

(singing softly)
I acted smart
And broke your heart
But now you're gone

They sit in silence and sip their drinks. Genevieve eats another Vienna Finger. After a while:

JENNY

When did he stop talking to you?

GENEVIEVE

It took a number of years.
He quieted down after a while.
He still talked to me, but in a gentler voice.
I think eventually he realized that he had punished me long enough.

Eventually *I* realized that I'd been punished long enough.
Okay, Jack. I'd say. I've been miserable for four whole years.
Can I be alone now?
I also promised him that I'd never marry anyone else.
And he listened and took me seriously and slowly slowly slowly he took his leave from me.

JENNY

Did you—
Did you ever marry someone else??

GENEVIEVE

No sir.

Pause.

JENNY

You / refused to—

GENEVIEVE

I wasn't interested anyway.

The grandfather clock chimes nine times. They listen.

GENEVIEVE

Nine o'clock.

MERTIS

That's late for you, Genevieve.

GENEVIEVE

That's very late for me.

Pause.

GENEVIEVE

(to Jenny)
Tell me your name again.

JENNY

Jenny.

GENEVIEVE

Jenny.
I should have remembered that.

Pause.

GENEVIEVE

Sometimes I still feel him.
Watching me.
Just a little.
A little glance now and again.
It's not so bad, though.
Sometimes it's bordering on pleasant.

Pause.

MERTIS

Do you ever feel watched, Jenny?

JENNY

Watched?

MERTIS

Like someone is watching you.
Watching over you.

JENNY

Um . . .

Pause.

JENNY

I don't think so.
I guess I'm not sure what / you—

MERTIS

What about when you were a child?

JENNY

Not by my parents?
By like . . . God?

MERTIS

Not your parents.
Just . . . a watcher.
A greater . . . a larger presence watching you from somewhere.

JENNY

I don't think so.

Pause.

JENNY

I mean, I guess I'm always thinking about how other people see me?
Like I'm picturing how I look to them.
And I'm always worried about . . . like I'm always worried about objects and what they're thinking? I'm always worried that they're unhappy. Elias thinks I have OCD.

MERTIS

What kind of objects?

JENNY

Well. All of them I guess. But when I was little I was always worried about my dolls. I had this one doll, um, Samantha, and I always felt like she was incredibly angry at me.

GENEVIEVE

Of course she was angry.

MERTIS

What do you mean, Genevieve?

GENEVIEVE

Angry to be a doll! To be a piece of plastic or glass and to be shaped into a human form and trapped! With one expression on your face! Frozen! People manhandling you.
And then put in a dress. Put in an itchy little dress!

JENNY

Yeah. Exactly. I felt like she was mad that she was a doll and mad at me for not doing a better job making her life as a doll easier. Sometimes I couldn't sleep at night because I could feel her thinking all these horrible thoughts about me. So I would um . . . oh my god I still feel bad about this . . . I would get up in the middle of the night and lock her in the kitchen cupboard. So I wouldn't feel her watching me. But then the next morning she'd be even more mad cuz she'd spent all night in the cupboard! And then I'd cry and beg her for forgiveness.

MERTIS

And would she forgive you?

JENNY

Nope. She never forgave me.

MERTIS

I always thought it would be a wonderful thing to be a doll.
To be . . .
To be free of responsibility.
To be able to provide joy to people without even moving.
Without even saying anything.

GENEVIEVE

You're dead wrong, Mertis. It's a terrible fate.

JENNY

And then when people gave me stuffed animals I would always feel like I was participating in some horrible like *system* . . . like I was running an orphanage and people kept dropping the animals off and I didn't have enough resources to provide for all of them and I knew most of them would get neglected and every time someone gave me one for like my birthday I would have this sinking feeling . . . like: oh god. Where is this one going to sleep tonight.

GENEVIEVE

It's no joke.

JENNY

But I'd also think, like, well at least it got me and not like Michelle who was this crazy sadistic girl on my block who would cut open her Cabbage Patch Dolls and put dog food inside of them.

MERTIS

I think they were lucky to have you.

JENNY

Now they're all in my mom's basement in Ohio.

GENEVIEVE

(ominously)
Cold.

JENNY

What?

GENEVIEVE

It's cold in the basement.

JENNY

Yeah.
It is.
My mom put them in plastic bags but then I transferred them to cardboard boxes last Thanksgiving and I carved out some little windows with a knife so they could peep out. She thought I was crazy.

Pause.

GENEVIEVE

Mertis takes very good care of her matter.

JENNY

Her what?

GENEVIEVE

Her matter.

Genevieve gestures around her at the room.

GENEVIEVE

Her matter! Her matter!

MERTIS

I try.

Mertis and Jenny gaze contemplatively around the room at all the matter.

GENEVIEVE

What are you doing?

MERTIS

We're looking at all the matter.

JENNY

I'm looking at a little angel playing guitar.

MERTIS

It's a lute, actually.

GENEVIEVE

Let me hold it.

Jenny gets up and picks up the angel and puts it in Genevieve's hands. Genevieve caresses the angel with great care and delicacy.

GENEVIEVE

Mmm.

Genevieve sets the angel in her lap like a baby.

JENNY

(to Genevieve)
Do you have children?

Genevieve ignores this question. Jenny tries to decide whether or not to repeat herself. She glances at Mertis who shakes her head no and draws a hand across her neck as if to say "don't ask again." Pause.

GENEVIEVE

(holding up a finger)
Did you hear that?

They all sit, listening. Then:

MERTIS

(quietly)
Hear what, Genevieve?

GENEVIEVE

It's that rustling sound again.

They all try to listen.

GENEVIEVE

A rustling or a whispering.
There!
No one heard it?

Jenny shakes her head no.

MERTIS

We can't hear it.

Pause.

GENEVIEVE

There!

Pause.

GENEVIEVE

. . . And there.

Pause.

GENEVIEVE

Nothing?

Pause.

JENNY

I don't hear anything.

GENEVIEVE

A rustling, a whispering, or possibly the beating of wings.

MERTIS

Genevieve thinks the house is haunted.

GENEVIEVE

You know it's haunted, Mertis.
You know it's capable of anything.

MERTIS

Didn't you hear that sound the other day?
Didn't you tell me you heard it at Price Chopper?

GENEVIEVE

You know this house is haunted.

MERTIS

Oh dear.
You're scaring my guest.

JENNY

No, no! I like um . . .
I like spooky things.
I like scary stories.

GENEVIEVE

There it is again.

Pause.

JENNY

I might be a tiny bit drunk.

Pause.

JENNY

It's making my cramps feel better though.

GENEVIEVE

(softly)
Since you're gone
The Wheel That Turns
The Fire That Burns . . .

JENNY

(to Mertis)
Is George going to join us?

MERTIS

I don't think so.
He's not feeling well.

JENNY

Oh no. Is / he—

MERTIS

He's been sick for a long time.

JENNY

I'm so sorry. What is—

MERTIS

We're not sure what it is.

Silence.

JENNY

Um . . .
Last summer I visited my friend in New Mexico and um . . .
we got drunk and smoked this really strong pot and we were
lying out on her deck looking at all the stars and um . . . I
don't know . . . the sky was so big that it seemed like it was
like um curving around me and I started feeling like the universe was . . .

They look at her.

JENNY

I felt like the universe was um—
Like the universe was having sex with me.
And it was really intense.
And I kind of . . . like . . . nothing like this has ever happened
to me before but . . .
I kind of had an orgasm.
Even though I wasn't even touching myself.

Pause.

JENNY

Um.
Wait.
Why did I tell you guys that?

Pause.

JENNY

Oh.
Because . . .
It wasn't really a Watcher or anything but it was like—
Yeah. I don't know if I felt Watched.
But I guess I felt—
Held.
And it like . . . somehow it was like an important thing.
In my life.

GENEVIEVE

How so.

JENNY

I felt . . .
I felt less alone being alone.
I mean I felt more lonely but less alone.
No. Sorry. More alone but less lonely.

Pause.

JENNY

Less alone in my alone-ness.

MERTIS

Oh yes.

GENEVIEVE

That's what they call a mystical experience.

JENNY

I guess.

Pause.

MERTIS

I just remembered a phrase but I don't remember who said it
or if I read it somewhere.
Forgive me if it was you Genevieve but it just keeps repeating
itself in my head and I'll be dipped if I know where I heard it.

GENEVIEVE

Say it.

MERTIS

Deep Calling Unto Deep.

Pause.

GENEVIEVE

Say it again.

MERTIS

Deep Calling Unto Deep.

JENNY

Deep Calling Unto Deep.

GENEVIEVE

That's definitely not me.

JENNY

Deep Calling Unto Deep.

MERTIS

Deep Calling Unto Deep.

JENNY

I don't know what it means but I like it.

Genevieve's phone sings a little song.

GENEVIEVE

Oop!
That's my nephew's ring.
He must be waiting for me outside.

Jenny looks at the phone.

JENNY

Joey?

GENEVIEVE

Mmhm.

Jenny runs over to the window.

JENNY

Does he drive a Chevy Impala?

GENEVIEVE

Very likely.
Time to go.

JENNY

But it's only 9!

GENEVIEVE

If I'm not asleep by 9:30 I fall into a deep despair.

Genevieve shakily gets up.

GENEVIEVE

Kitty, I love you very much.

MERTIS

I love you darling Genevieve.

Genevieve thrusts her hand out for Jenny to shake.
Jenny rushes to meet it.

GENEVIEVE

Jenny it was a pleasure meeting you.
I hope your love affair with the universe continues.

JENNY

Oh, thanks!
Yeah.
Um.
It was so great meeting you.
I hope we um . . .

MERTIS

(to Genevieve)
I'll walk you out.

They walk out, arm in arm.
Jenny sits at the table, a little drunk and dreamy.
Suddenly all the lights on the Christmas tree go out.
Jenny doesn't notice at first. The room looks different but she isn't
sure why.
Then she turns around and sees that the lights are out.
She gets up.
She wanders around the parlor looking for the plug and the outlet.
She finally finds them. Maybe this involves getting a little tangled
up in the tree.
The cord is still plugged in. She unplugs the cord and then plugs it
in again.
The tree lights up.
Then three seconds later the lights go out again.
Jenny stands there, befuddled.
After a second, she turns and regards Samantha on the landing.

JENNY

. . . Sorry.

Mertis reenters.

JENNY

The Christmas lights went out.

Mertis turns on a little fake Tiffany lamp near the front door.

JENNY

Um . . . can I ask . . . how long have you had that doll?

She points to the landing.

MERTIS

American Girl Doll Samantha?

JENNY

Yeah.

MERTIS

I don't remember.
Hmm.
Let's see.
When did Samantha come into my life.
I'm not sure.
Maybe she was a gift from someone?

They look at Samantha.

MERTIS

Isn't she pretty?

JENNY

Yeah.
I had the same . . .

That's the same one I had when I was a kid.
That's the one I was talking about.

MERTIS

Really?
Why didn't you say so before?

JENNY

. . . I don't know.

Jenny touches her stomach.

JENNY

My cramps just came back.

MERTIS

Do you want to lie down again?

JENNY

Yeah.

Jenny waddles over to the couch and lies in a fetal position.

MERTIS

Would you like some chocolate tea?

JENNY

That's a real thing?

*Mertis walks over to the snack/teakettle nook and holds up the box
of tea bags.*

MERTIS

Red Velvet Cuppa Chocolate Tea.
It's a perfect substitute when you're craving sugary desserts.

> JENNY

... Sure.

Pause. Mertis puts the electric kettle on to boil. About ten seconds pass.

> JENNY

Do you know any stories?

> MERTIS

Made-up stories?

Jenny nods.

> MERTIS

I don't know if I can make up a story.

> JENNY

It's okay.

> MERTIS

Hmmm ...

The electric kettle starts making its slow way toward a boil. Throughout the following Mertis picks two mugs and puts two chocolate tea bags in them.

> MERTIS

Let's see ...
Maybe I can tell you ...
Mmm.
Do you know what I did last week?

> JENNY

What.

> MERTIS

I memorized all the different things you can call a group of birds.

JENNY

Wait, what do you mean?

MERTIS

For instance.
A gaggle of geese.

JENNY

Ohhhhh.

MERTIS

A congress of crows.
A convocation of eagles.
A team of ducks.
I bet you already know that one.
A tiding of magpies.
A colony of gulls.
A host of sparrows.
A cast of falcons.
Isn't that nice? A cast?

Jenny nods and lies back on the couch, her knees to her chest.

MERTIS

A company of parrots.
A concentration of kingfishers.
A siege of herons.
A wisdom of owls.
A mustering of storks.
A dule of doves.
A sedge of cranes.
A cover of coots.

JENNY

Wow.
I can't believe you memorized all of these.

MERTIS

I love em.
I love em.
Let's see.
A raft of loons.
A pride of penguins.
A troubling of hummingbirds.
A bevy of quail.
Mmmm . . .
A charm of finches . . .
An exaltation of larks.
Ooh yes.
That's my favorite.
An exaltation of larks.

The Christmas tree lights flicker back on.

MERTIS

Look at that.

The water reaches a boil. Mertis pours the tea. She walks over to the couch. They sit together with their mugs.

MERTIS

How long have you been seeing Elias?

JENNY

Um . . . a little over three years? If you don't count—
Yeah.
How long have you and George been together?

MERTIS

Thirteen years.

JENNY

Thirteen years. Wow. That's . . .
Wait. I guess that's not / actually—

MERTIS

At my age it's not that long.

JENNY

Yeah. Right.

MERTIS

I was married to someone else for twenty-five.

The sound of the porch door opening. Boots stamping. The front door opens. Elias comes in, bundled up.

ELIAS

(to Jenny)
Hi.
(to Mertis)
Hi Kitty.

MERTIS

Hello Elias.

ELIAS

(to Jenny)
How are you feeling?

JENNY

Bad.

ELIAS

I'm so sorry.
That sucks.

Pause.

ELIAS

(looking at the table)
Pinot Grigio.
Nice.

JENNY

How was the ghost tour?

ELIAS

Oh.

Ludicrous.

Entertaining.

The tour guide was this woman named "Spooky."

He holds out his wrist.

ELIAS

I got a free bracelet.

JENNY

Cool.

MERTIS

Did you see any ghosts?

ELIAS

Well.

So.

We met in a parking lot and Spooky took us through a grave-yard and then down this alleyway where like they used to dump a lot of dead soldier bodies or something and we had these like beeper sticks that would go off if they sensed like "ghost energy" or whatever and it was starting to feel pretty lame but then she took us to the Farnsworth / House?

MERTIS

Oh, the Farnsworth House. Yes, / that's—

ELIAS

And then she just let us like roam around on our own and take pictures. And anyway. I went upstairs and into this like antiquey like kid's bedroom? Like apparently a kid lived there in the nineteenth century and they kept all his stuff or something. And anyway I just took a picture of the room because it was kind of cool to see a nineteenth century like little kid's bed but THEN after I left I looked at the photo and . . .

He takes out his phone and shows the photo to them.

JENNY

I can't see.

Elias hands the phone to her. She and Mertis look at it.

ELIAS

See the blurry area?

JENNY

Where.

ELIAS

On the left.

MERTIS

Oh yes.

JENNY

I don't see it.

MERTIS

Right there. Near the window.

JENNY

Oh yeah.

ELIAS

It's like a *ghostly blur.*
And it totally wasn't there when I was standing in the room.

They all stare the photo.

ELIAS

Anyway. I showed it to Spooky and she was psyched.
She wants me to email it to her.

*Jenny's phone dings in her pocket. Jenny hands Elias's phone back
to Elias and takes her phone out of her pocket for a brief glance
before she sticks it back into her pocket.*

ELIAS

Who was that.

JENNY

My sister.

ELIAS

What'd she say?

JENNY

Oh. She bought a—it's a long story. She bought a lottery ticket
for this thing.
I'll tell you later.

A weird pause.

MERTIS

(partly to fill the silence)
This house was a hospital.

ELIAS

During the battle?

MERTIS

Mmhm.
The man who sold it to me told me that—oh this isn't a very
pleasant story.

ELIAS	JENNY
Tell us! Tell us!	Yes please tell us.

MERTIS

Well. It was a hospital for Union soldiers and the story goes that, you know, they had to do quite a few amputations and there wasn't an easy way to get rid of . . . to get rid of the limbs during the chaos of the battle so they would . . . they would throw them out the window.
Oh dear.
So the story is that there were so many piles of arms and legs outside the windows . . .
   (she gestures around the living room)
. . . that you couldn't see in or out.
They went ten feet high.

They all sit and visualize the arms outside the windows.

ELIAS

So what have you ladies been up to tonight?

JENNY

We were talking about birds.

ELIAS

Glad I missed it.

MERTIS

Jenny says you don't like birds.

ELIAS

Yup.

MERTIS

May I ask why?

JENNY

Oh god.
He's / gonna—

ELIAS

They look like little evil robot dinosaurs?
They have sharp little beaks they could poke your eyes out with?
They crap on you? They eat trash?

JENNY

He's actually extremely scared of them.

ELIAS

If they get too close. If a pigeon gets too close to me I get very
weird. A rat is somehow considered dirty. But a bird . . . people
romanticize birds.

MERTIS

Oh yes.
I romanticize birds very much.

They absorb this.

JENNY

Maybe something bad happened to you when you were a kid.
Like involving a bird.

ELIAS

A lot of bad stuff happened to me when I was a kid but it
didn't involve any birds.

JENNY

Elias's dad ran the Hostetter Institute in California? Have you
heard of it?

MERTIS	ELIAS
I'm not sure.	Where are you going with this?

JENNY

It's near Big Sur . . . it's like the most beautiful place in the world and it's like this crazy institute where you can go take like um Sufi spinning classes or do like crazy Gestalt seminars and there are / these—

ELIAS

It's a retreat center.

JENNY

—there are these amazing hot springs and these like hot tubs built into the rocks. It's one of the reasons people go there. Anyway everyone is always naked and like sitting around in the outdoor tubs and anyway this one time when Elias was really little, / like really little—

ELIAS

What story are you telling?

JENNY

—he was sitting in one of the tubs with his mom and dad, this is when they were still together, / and there was this GUY in the tub with them, one of the guests, and he—

ELIAS

Jenny.
JENNY!

JENNY

—asked if he could kiss Elias because Elias was such a beautiful little boy and his parents said yes and this man kissed Elias. On the mouth.

Pause.

MERTIS

Oh my.

A long silence. Elias stands there. Jenny bites her thumbnail. She is gleeful and still tipsy but also terrified.

ELIAS

I'm.

Um.

Okay.

Thank you.

JENNY

That was one of the bad things he was talking about. There weren't a lot of / boundaries and—

ELIAS

Um.

Okay.

Speaking of boundaries.

Okay.

So.

At times like this.

At times like this the fact that you tell me that you don't have very very deep wells of rage towards me is so obviously um laid bare as a huge whopping lie because I have no idea why you would tell the owner of our bed-and- / breakfast—

JENNY

You were talking about / bad things that—

ELIAS

—about something that happened to me as a small child. Something extremely personal that I didn't tell you until after we had been dating *for over a year.*

Pause.

JENNY

I just thought . . .

Pause.

ELIAS

You have so much anger towards me, Jenny.

JENNY

I don't. / I just—

ELIAS

Please.
Please.
Just . . . just think about the anger you have towards me and then when you want to talk about that anger explicitly instead lying to me and fucking with my head then feel free to come talk to me.

Elias walks toward the stairs, then stops for a second as if to consider saying something else.

JENNY

Eli.

He walks up the stairs and is gone.
A silence. Jenny sips her tea, not making eye contact. Finally:

JENNY

This really does taste like chocolate.

MERTIS

You should probably go talk to him.

JENNY

. . . Yeah.

Jenny doesn't move.

JENNY

It's just . . .
We almost broke up a few weeks ago so things are a little . . .

MERTIS

Oh.

JENNY

He's still upset.

MERTIS

Mm.

JENNY

I guess we're um . . . we're trying to um . . . heal?
But I keep making him mad.
He always thinks I'm lying.

Jenny starts to tear up.

JENNY

Sorry.

MERTIS

Oh dear. No, I'm sorry.

Jenny looks toward the landing.

JENNY

He's gonna wanna have a fight and I don't wanna have a fight.

Pause.

JENNY

Okay.

She gets up and shuffles up the stairs. When she reaches the landing:

MERTIS

Jenny.

Jenny turns around.

MERTIS

Did you ever think about giving Samantha away?

JENNY

Nope. I saved up two years' worth of babysitting money to buy her.

Pause.

JENNY

Thanks for the wine.

MERTIS

Oh you're welcome.
Do you want to take the rest of the bottle upstairs?
Share it with Elias?
I don't drink.

JENNY

No, that's okay.

Jenny shuffles up the stairs.
Mertis stands alone in the parlor.
She is looking at the bottle of wine. It is looking back at her.
Faint and muffled from upstairs: we can just make this out:

ELIAS

Just admit it! Remember when we were stoned / and—

JENNY

No! I don't!! We were stoned!!

ELIAS

You said all this incredibly mean shit and then / claimed—

JENNY

Could you please lower your voice??

He lowers his voice. There is nothing else to hear.
Mertis continues her silent eye contact with the white wine. Eventually she downs her glass of water, walks over to the wine bottle, and refills her glass. Then she takes the glass of white wine and exits into her area through the French doors. On her way out she turns on the little jukebox radio and changes the clock's hands to 12:04. Bach's Cello Suite IV-Sarabande fills the room.

Scene Two

12:04 A.M.
Bach's Cello Suite IV-Sarabande is still playing.
Everything is dark except for the lights on the Christmas tree.
Jenny comes down the stairs wrapped in her quilt.
She walks to and stands in front of Mertis's set of French doors.
She hesitates, then knocks.
No answer.
She knocks again.
Then she walks over to the player piano and sits on the bench.
She holds her hands an inch above the keyboard as if she's about to play.
Elias comes down and stands on the landing.
Jenny looks up at him, her hands still above the piano keys.
He walks over to her.

JENNY

Feel my hands.

He feels them.

ELIAS

Yeesh.

Jenny sticks one hand under his shirt and tries to touch his stomach.

ELIAS

Auggghh!! Stop! They're fucking freezing!

She looks at her fingers.

JENNY

They won't warm up.
    (referring to the French doors)
I wonder if she's asleep or ignoring me.
I guess George is ignoring me too.

ELIAS

Who's George?

JENNY

Mertis has a husband.

ELIAS

Who doesn't live here?

JENNY

No! He lives here!
George. They've been married for thirteen years.

ELIAS

Why haven't we seen him?

JENNY

She said something about him being sick.

ELIAS

Are you sure George exists?

JENNY

Oh come on.

Elias walks over to the window and looks out.

ELIAS

It's so weird.
I can't imagine living here.
I can't imagine just like . . .
Being A Person Who Lives in Gettysburg Pennsylvania.
Like, oh hey, my name's George, I'm seventy-three years old and
I live in Gettysburg Pennsylvania. I Run a Bed-and-Breakfast
in Gettysburg Pennsylvania.

Jenny just looks at him.

ELIAS

What?

JENNY

I can imagine it.
I can imagine being anyone.

ELIAS

We're probably talking about two different things.

*He walks over and sits on the couch and puts his fingers on his
temples.*

JENNY

What's wrong?

He doesn't respond.

JENNY

Was that a brain zap?

He nods.

JENNY

Poor baby.

ELIAS

Please don't call me a poor baby.

Elias takes his glasses off and puts them on the couch next to them.
He keeps rubbing his temples.
Jenny walks over and starts massaging the back of his neck.
He shakes his head no.
She removes her hand.
She picks up his glasses and puts them on.

JENNY

I always forget how strong your prescription is.

She holds her hand out in front of her.

JENNY

My hand is so small.
Everything is so small.

She wanders around the room.
Elias continues to rub his temples, tormented.

ELIAS

Did he have like perfect eyesight or something?

Jenny turns around.
Pause.

JENNY

John?

Pause.

JENNY

I don't know.
    (short pause)
Maybe he was wearing contacts.

ELIAS

. . . And he had a huge cock?

Jenny just stands there, blinking behind his glasses.
Elias tries to breathe. After a long silence:

ELIAS

You know what?
I changed my mind.

Pause.

ELIAS

I want to know the number.

Pause.

JENNY

Okay.

ELIAS

And don't say "three times" or something if it was five times.
Just tell me it was five times.

Pause.

JENNY

    (still wearing his glasses)
I'm not sure I know the exact number.

ELIAS

Give me an approximate number.

JENNY

Um.
(pause)
Twenty . . .
(horrible pause, the weight of this, then:)
. . . Two?

Another silence.

JENNY

That includes everything. Like every time we . . .
I wouldn't have sex for the first few months. I wouldn't even
let myself come. I just waited for / him to—

ELIAS

You just serviced him.

Pause.

ELIAS

And that made you feel better about yourself?
Acting like a prostitute made you feel like a good person?

JENNY

Most of the time I didn't even want to be there.

ELIAS

So then why'd / you—

JENNY

Because he wanted me and he said he needed me and I felt
guilty saying / no to—

ELIAS

You felt guilty saying no to him?!

JENNY

He would call me crying and beg / me to—

ELIAS

And that meant you / had to—

JENNY

I'm trying to be honest!
You never cry. I felt / like he—

ELIAS

I do so fucking cry!

JENNY

You cry when you listen to that Bob Dylan song.
I never make you cry. .
And he would tell me he loved me and he would look at me
for hours and—
I would come home and I wouldn't bother you and you'd
seem so *relieved.* Just to go to bed and not have to touch me.

Jenny weeps.

JENNY

It felt like he cast a spell on me.
But it's over.
I'll never do anything like that ever again.
I want to kill myself when I think about it.
I want to kill myself when I think about what a terrible per-
son I am.

Elias watches her weep.

ELIAS

Well.
You win.
You're crying again and I'm the dry-eyed sociopath.

JENNY

(still crying)
You can hit me.
You can punch me in the face.

ELIAS

Oh my god. Jenny.

JENNY

Just punch me in the face.

ELIAS

I am not going to punch you in the face.

JENNY

Yell at me.

ELIAS

You hate when I yell at you.
You tell me I'm yelling when I speak in a normal tone of voice.

JENNY

This time you can yell at me.

ELIAS

You don't even understand what yelling is.
You / think—

JENNY

You can do it. I'm giving you permission to do it.

Pause.

ELIAS

It would scare the shit out of you.
If I yelled at you the way my family yelled at me you'd fucking run for the hills.

JENNY

Show me.

Pause.

JENNY

You can show me.
Maybe then I'll understand.
Maybe then we'll both feel better.

Pause.

JENNY

It can be like—
It can be a demonstration.
Just like a demonstration.
Because I think we just have different definitions / of—

Elias gets up in her face. He's not touching her at all but he's an inch away from her. The following is truly scary and ugly. Maybe a few flecks of spit hit her face.

ELIAS

THIS IS FUCKING YELLING.
THIS IS WHAT YELLING LOOKS LIKE.
THIS IS WHAT I MEAN WHEN I SAY YELLING.

Jenny remains absolutely still throughout this, still wearing his glasses.
When he's done Elias stares at her, breathless.
Jenny is still and expressionless.
Elias sits down.
He looks at her, then looks away. After a while:

ELIAS

You're not gonna say anything?

She still doesn't move.
Nothing.

ELIAS

Oh my god.
I like totally traumatized you.

More silence. He's in agony.

ELIAS

Jenny.

Jenny finally blinks.

JENNY

I'm okay.

ELIAS

No you're not.

Jenny takes off his glasses.

JENNY

I'm okay.

Pause. She gives him back his glasses.
He puts them on, uncomfortably.

JENNY

I'm fine.

ELIAS

I feel humiliated.

JENNY

You shouldn't.

Elias turns, walks up the stairs and disappears upstairs.
Jenny sits alone on the couch.
After a minute, he walks back downstairs, grabs her, throws her
down, pins her hands, and starts kissing her. She kisses him back,
desperately.
They keep kissing but after a minute Elias suddenly schlumps over
in a heap on the other side of the sofa.

JENNY

What just happened?

ELIAS

(not looking at her)
I feel too depressed.

JENNY

That's okay.

ELIAS

I might need to go back on the Cymbalta.

JENNY

That's okay.

Pause.

ELIAS

I want to sleep alone tonight.

JENNY

. . . Okay.

Pause.

JENNY

But where do I—

ELIAS

You're warmer down here anyway, right?

After a second, she nods.
Elias gets up and walks back upstairs. She waits for him to come back. He doesn't. The Christmas tree lights flicker off, then on again, and then off again.
Jenny looks at them.
Then she looks at Samantha.

End of Act Two
Intermission Two

Except:

A minute after the lights come up on the audience Genevieve slowly feels her way out from behind the curtain and gropes her way to the edge of stage.

GENEVIEVE

Hello. Hello.

She teeters on the edge of the stage, almost falling off.

GENEVIEVE

Don't go yet.
Stay five more minutes.
I'm going to tell you a story but I'm going to do it in under five minutes.
Does someone have a watch?
    (if no one responds immediately)
Does someone have a watch?

She waits for someone to shout "yes." Then:

GENEVIEVE

All right. Good.

So you'll time me and when five minutes are up you'll shout STOP and then I'll stop. All right?

All right?

And then you can take a little break and go to the bathroom. All right.

When I went mad I went mad in seven stages!

One: I dreamt of scorpions every night for a month. Scorpions crawling closer and closer to me across the floor. Every night a little closer.

Two: I kept hearing a name inside my head. Paluba? Ich—Irck—Stack—Irkewicz. Ichthyowitz. Irkthowicz. Irkthy . . . kowcowicz. Icktho—Irzykowcowicz. Irzykowski. I'd never heard this name before in my life.

Three: one morning I awoke to the sensation that the scorpions were now inside my head. I felt them moving around, rooting through my brain matter. Occasionally they would bite me but only when I angered them.

Four: I noticed that my breasts were slowly shrinking and that a tiny penis was growing between my legs. I knew that God was doing some kind of experiment on me but I could not figure out what that experiment was. I prayed it was all for the best.

Five: the scorpions in my head disappeared but they were replaced two weeks later by the knowledge that tiny men were colonizing my brain. Workers. They were drawing up some sort of plan, chatting, drawing lines across my skull. At one point two hundred Benedictine monks entered my right ear, took a tour of my head, and then exited out the left.

Six: I became aware of an unus mundus.

I felt a deep but also disturbing connection with the soul of every person and every object that had ever existed. Not just the souls of departed conquistadors but also the soul of a picture frame, a toy trumpet. Sometimes I could see souls or sense souls but I also became able to taste and smell souls.

Seven: I realized that this was all the work of my ex-husband, not God. I became aware that he had replaced God in the celestial sphere. There had been some kind of battle between John and God and John had won. I was now in a godless world. John's world. I had a vision of God's soul, a dead soul, the corpse of a soul, floating down a muddy river.

Pause.

GENEVIEVE

I went mad and then I was forty-five, which was older than I thought I'd ever be, and then I was fifty, which was older than I thought I'd ever be when I was forty-five, and then on the night of my fifty-seventh birthday I went blind and I stood naked in the middle of my bedroom and all of a sudden I was at the center of the universe, facing out. No more trying to get in anyone else's head. Oh, what does she think of me? What does that man bagging my groceries think of—nope. It's just me! Alone in the universe! Standing in the center of my own life. I can't even look in a mirror. It's just me and my thoughts and sometimes I have no thoughts at all. Sometimes I just lie in bed in the morning and think about nothing.

Imagine that.

Before you take a break, imagine that.

Sitting in the center of your own life with no thoughts at all about what other people are thinking.

They can think whatever they like.

You can all think whatever you like about me.

(to the person timing her)

See? And it hasn't even been five minutes.

She exits, finding her way back to the opening in the curtain. And now Intermission Two really begins.

Act Three

———

Scene One

Morning. No music.
Elias is sitting in Paris at one of the little round tables waiting for
breakfast.
He is bored.
After a while he spots Mertis's notebook. He walks over to it and
starts flipping through it. He frowns and starts reading the words
out loud. Slowly, carefully, trying them out as if they were spells:

ELIAS

satyabasanam karoti
rajanicara
putri
vastra putrika.
angakok
paksini
paluba

The player piano spontaneously starts playing "Me and My Shadow." Simultaneously, the French doors to Mertis's wing of the house fly open and Mertis comes out, a bit disheveled.

MERTIS

(over the music)
Good morning!

ELIAS

. . . Hi.

MERTIS

I overslept!
I'll start making breakfast right now!

ELIAS

No rush.

Mertis exits again. Elias watches the player piano as it plays its way through "Me and My Shadow."
Mertis comes out of the French doors again and tiptoes over to the jukebox CD player. She turns it on and Bach's chorus (BWV 243) from Magnificat in D Major starts playing. Mertis starts to exit, then remembers something else and hurries over to the grandfather clock, which is still operating on the time from Act Two. She sets the clock to the correct hour, 9:08, and then hurries off again, back through the French doors.
Elias watches all of this.
Then he walks over and looks through the pile of newspapers on the coffee table.
They are the same as the day before.
Elias looks up at the landing, waiting for Jenny to appear.
Mertis rushes out of the French doors again with little boxes of cereal and a little pitcher of milk and a few bananas under her arm.
She heaves them onto the cupboard.

MERTIS

I'm frying up some pancake batter right now.

Mertis starts to exit again. Elias points to the notebook.

ELIAS

What language is that?

Mertis stops and looks.

ELIAS

In that notebook.

MERTIS

What do you mean?

Elias picks up the notebook and reads:

ELIAS

"Bhojanam samyak . . . karoti cet bhavatim kridanakam dadami."

MERTIS

. . . I don't know.
I don't know whose book that is.
Maybe Genevieve left it here.

She starts walking toward the French doors again.

ELIAS

Who's Genevieve?

Mertis doesn't answer, seeming not to hear, and disappears.
Elias sits at one of the tables.
He waits.
After a minute he takes out his iPhone, searches through it, and then starts playing Bob Dylan's "I Want You" through the tiny little iPhone speaker. It sounds kind of terrible mixed with the Bach coming from the jukebox. He holds his phone up to his ear. When Dylan starts to sing the line "Your dancing child/With his Chinese suit/He spoke to me/I took his flute/I wasn't very cute to him/Was I," Elias

tears up. Shortly after Mertis enters with a plate of pancakes and a pitcher of coffee. Elias turns his phone off.

MERTIS

(a little breathless)
Blueberry pancakes.

ELIAS

Thanks.

MERTIS

Is Jenny still asleep?

ELIAS

Um. Yeah. I don't know.
I think she ended up sleeping in the Jackson room last night.
I hope that's okay.

Mertis is slightly alarmed but tries not to show it.

MERTIS

She's still up there?

ELIAS

Yeah. Sorry. We can pay—we're happy to pay / for—

MERTIS

No, no.
I just . . .

Mertis wavers on her feet, trying to decide whether or not to go upstairs to check on Jenny.

ELIAS

She'll come down soon.
Um.

I think we're probably gonna leave this afternoon instead of tomorrow morning.
You can keep / the—

MERTIS

Is there something wrong with the house?

ELIAS

No. We just—

MERTIS

I thought you still wanted to do the rest of the battlefield and the Cyclorama!

ELIAS

We do, / but—

MERTIS

Are you switching to another bed-and-breakfast?

ELIAS

No. No.
We're having some problems.
I mean me and Jenny. And—
It has nothing to do with—
You've been great.

MERTIS

I see.

She gazes at him sympathetically.

MERTIS

Do you want some cream with your coffee?

ELIAS

Yes. Please.

Mertis exits and then reenters with a little creamer pot in the shape
of an animal head, preferably a dog.
Elias pours the cream into his coffee.
Mertis hovers.

MERTIS

Did she . . .
The Jackson room was unlocked?

ELIAS

I guess so.
I'm really sorry.
We'll pay you the / extra—

MERTIS

No no no.

Elias miserably eats his pancakes and sips his coffee while she watches
him.

MERTIS

I'm just going to check on one thing upstairs.

ELIAS

(his mouth full)
Okay.

Mertis makes her way slowly upstairs.
Then some very faint and very strange sounds from a room upstairs.
Maybe the beating of wings.
After a minute or two, Mertis comes back down.

MERTIS

She's fast asleep.

ELIAS

You checked on her?

MERTIS

Yes. I was just concerned because as I said before the Jackson has a leak in the ceiling and is . . . it's just a . . . it's just an odd little room and I wanted to make sure Jenny was all right.

They sit. He eats.
She watches him.

MERTIS

Is there anything else I can do?

ELIAS

No.
Thanks.

Mertis nods and starts tidying up around Elias. She puts the porcelain angel back in her proper place on the shelf. She notices a wine glass from the night before. She picks it up. Elias chews his food, then becomes self-conscious about the sound of his chewing and stops.

ELIAS

Do you . . .
Have there been times in your life when . . .

A pause while he thinks about how to say this.

ELIAS

Have you ever been in something and just like had no idea whether you should go or stay? And just like wished for like a . . . for like a sign? Just for someone to say: GO. Or: STAY. Like for God to come down from the sky and be like . . . "Do *that.*"

Pause.

MERTIS

Yes.
Yes I have been in that situation.

Pause.

MERTIS

I was married for a long time to somebody and I felt that way
during the last fifteen years of our marriage.

ELIAS

So did you go or did you stay?

MERTIS

I should have gone.
But I stayed.
And then he died.

ELIAS

Oh. Wow.
I'm sorry.

She nods.

ELIAS

Did he um . . . what did he die of?

MERTIS

It's . . . oh it's a terrible story.
I don't want to disturb you.

ELIAS

I won't be disturbed.

MERTIS

I won't go into the gory details.
But.
He was building . . . he was building a kind of . . . a kind of
contraption in the basement and he electrocuted himself.

ELIAS
(this is not what he was expecting)
. . . Huh.

Pause.

ELIAS

What kind of / contrap—

MERTIS

You've been feeling that way about Jenny?
Like you don't know whether to go or stay?

ELIAS

Yeah.
And she always wants to stay. She's always like, totally com-
mitted to it.
But then she lies to me.

Pause.

ELIAS

I mean, she lied about some really big stuff. And then I found
out.
But what's weird is that I also catch her in these totally dumb
unnecessary lies that have nothing to do with anything.

Pause.

ELIAS

I mean, I'm not saying I'm such a good person.
But I don't lie.
I don't get the point of lying.
Like if I don't tell Jenny the truth I actually feel like I'm gonna
go insane.
So I just have no idea what like makes a good . . .
I have no idea how people decide to stay or go.

.   MERTIS

Are you in love with her?

ELIAS

Uh . . .

Yeah.

I mean.

I love her.

But I don't know the difference between loving someone and being in love with someone unless it's the difference between being together for three years or three months.

Maybe I've never been in love with anyone.

I don't know.

He starts eating his pancakes again. Mouth full:

ELIAS

I've always had this problem.

Every girl I've dated . . . after a few months . . .

I look at them and they start to seem like . . .

I start to think of them as, uh . . . like as an insect.

MERTIS

What kind of insect?

ELIAS

Like the big green insects that land on your screen door at night.

MERTIS

Praying mantis?

ELIAS

Maybe.

Those weird green insects.

With their bellies pressed up against the screen.

Staring at you. Trying to get in.

Pause.

ELIAS

Anyway with Jenny the insect thing didn't happen at first.
And I was really excited, like, maybe it's over.
But then it did happen. After we'd been dating for a year.
But that was still an improvement.

Pause.

ELIAS

And I don't think of her as an insect *all* the time.
It's not like I always look at her and see an insect face.
Just . . . sometimes.

MERTIS

I think I know what you mean.

ELIAS

Really?

MERTIS

Yes. I remember with my ex-husband I would look at him
from a certain angle and he would seem to be a terrible sort
of prehistoric fish.

ELIAS

Ha.

MERTIS

And sometimes George looks to me like a woodland—
Like a marmot or a woodchuck.

ELIAS

George is your husband?

She nods.

MERTIS

Maybe looking at someone every day makes them seem a bit creature-like.

(short pause)

The way when you look at a word for too long it doesn't seem like a word anymore.

ELIAS

Yeah.

MERTIS

It probably helps if you don't mind the animal. For instance I greatly prefer a woodchuck to a prehistoric fish.

ELIAS

Right.

MERTIS

How do you feel about green insects?

ELIAS

I guess they're not so bad.

MERTIS

They're not as bad as birds.

He laughs.

ELIAS

Yeah. They're not as bad as birds.

MERTIS

So at least you're not in a relationship with a bird.

For some reason this troubles Elias. After a silence:

MERTIS

Did you feel watched as a child, Elias?

ELIAS

Watched?

MERTIS

Like there was someone watching over you.
An unseen presence.

Pause.

ELIAS

Uh . . .
I mean . . .
. . . Yeah.

MERTIS

You did?

ELIAS

Sure.

MERTIS

Did it feel / like a—

ELIAS

It was like . . . yeah.

Pause.

ELIAS

A Watcher.
Yeah.

MERTIS

Do you remember when you felt it for the first time?

ELIAS

Uh . . .

I guess since I can remember?

I mean what Jenny failed to mention last night is that hot tub thing is my first memory.

My very first memory.

So . . .

He was definitely there. Watching that.

Watching over me.

Pause.

ELIAS

Uh . . . sorry. I actually feel weird talking about it because I've never talked about it before and I feel like I'm not supposed to.

Pause.

MERTIS

The Watcher doesn't want you to talk about him?

It's a him?

ELIAS

Yeah.

Or like . . . you're just . . . you're not supposed to . . .

It's like sacred . . . secret . . . stuff.

He shudders.

ELIAS

I don't know.

Doesn't everyone feel like there's a Watcher?

MERTIS

I don't think so.

ELIAS

Did *you* feel like that when you were a kid? Watched?

MERTIS

Oh yes.

ELIAS

And did you think that was God?

MERTIS

Yes.

Pause.

MERTIS

I have one more question.
I hope you don't mind.

ELIAS

Okay.

MERTIS

Did you feel like on some level he was taking care of you?

ELIAS

Yeah.
Uh.
I felt like he was watching and seeing and uh . . . yeah. When good stuff happened I felt like he was giving it to me as a reward for making it through the bad stuff.
But then when bad stuff happened . . . I mean, when bad stuff still happens . . . I wonder if he's punishing me for being an asshole.

Pause.

ELIAS

I sound like a religious—
I mean, I'm not religious at all.
I come from a family of Jewish atheists.

Pause.

ELIAS

I feel really weird now.

MERTIS

You're worried he's going to be mad at you?

ELIAS

. . . Yeah.

Elias starts to feel overwhelmed by something.

ELIAS

I'm um . . .

Pause.

ELIAS

Are you . . . why did you ask me that?
Are you Christian or something?

MERTIS

I'm a Neoplatonist.

The doorbell rings.

ELIAS

I don't know what that means.

MERTIS

Oh dear.
That's Genevieve.
She's here for her weekly reading.

ELIAS

That's cool.
I don't think I want to talk about this anymore.

Elias stands up.

ELIAS

I'm gonna go wake up Jenny.

He walks up the stairs. Mertis starts to walk toward the front door.
Elias stops on the landing.

ELIAS

What did you mean, odd?

Pause.

ELIAS

When you were talking about the Jackson room.

MERTIS

Oh.

ELIAS

Is this house, like, haunted or something?

MERTIS

No. I don't think it's haunted.
It just has a lot of history.

ELIAS

. . . Like the arms outside of the window.

MERTIS

Yes. Like that.
And it's just a strange little place.
It's been very good to me.
But sometimes it takes on a life of its own.

ELIAS

What does that mean?

MERTIS

Oh, I've had the experience of certain rooms . . .
Certain rooms being somewhat unreliable on certain nights.

The doorbell rings again.

ELIAS

/ Like—

MERTIS

But the Chamberlain is very reliable and that's why I was
happy for you and Jenny to sleep in it. The Jackson can be a
little temperamental. But it's fine right now. The door is there
and it's unlocked and she's sleeping like a baby. I'm sorry.
I have to let Genevieve in out of the cold.

She exits into the foyer. Elias walks back upstairs.

Scene Two

The day passes. The winter sun crosses the sky and then eventually sets in strange colors and all is dark.

During this transition Mertis and Genevieve sit in the parlor while Mertis reads out loud to Genevieve from a dusty copy of H. P. Love-craft's "The Call of Cthulhu." Mertis is reading by the daylight but by the very end of the reading she is reading in the dark.

MERTIS

"Old Castro remembered bits of hideous legend that paled the speculations of theosophists and made man and the world seem recent and transient indeed. There had been aeons when other Things ruled the earth, and They had had great cities. Remains of Them, he said the deathless Chinamen had told him, were still to be found as Cyclopean stones on islands in the Pacific. They all died vast epochs of time before men came, but there were arts which could revive Them when the stars had come round again to the right positions in the cycle of eternity. They had, indeed, come themselves from the stars, and brought Their images with Them.

These Great Old Ones, Castro continued, were not composed altogether of flesh and blood. They had shape—for did not this star-fashioned image prove it?—but that shape was not made of matter. When the stars were right, They could plunge from world to world through the sky; but when the stars were wrong, They could not live. But although They no longer lived, They would never really die. They all lay in stone houses in Their great city of R'lyeh, preserved by the spells of mighty Cthulhu for a glorious resurrection when the stars and the earth might once more be ready for Them. But at that time some force from outside must serve to liberate Their bodies. The spells that preserved Them intact likewise prevented Them from making an initial move, and They could only lie awake in the dark and think whilst uncounted millions of years rolled by. They knew all that was occurring, but Their mode of speech was transmitted thought. Even now They talked in Their tombs . . ."

It is completely dark now, except for the lights on the Christmas tree.
Mertis gets up and lights a few candles.
She changes the time on the grandfather clock.
Then she clears the dishes from breakfast and brings them through the French doors into her wing of the house.
She does not return.
Genevieve remains in the shadows, invisible.

Scene Three

The sound of the car pulling up and the door slamming.
Elias and Jenny enter. They see that the parlor is candlelit and empty.

ELIAS

No music.

Jenny ignores this and heads for the stairs.

ELIAS

I see.
You silently suffered through Pickett's Charge and the Visitors
Center and now you can't wait to get out of here.

Jenny stops on the landing, exhausted, her back to him. Elias walks
up to the landing. He stands behind her and puts his arms around
her. She's frozen still.

ELIAS

You're like a statue.

He lifts her arm and it flops back down.
He lifts a strand of her hair up and it flops back down.
He wraps his arms around her waist.
He picks her up and then puts her back down.
Maybe she cracks a tiny smile.
He picks her up and carries her, stiffly, like a mannequin, down to the couch and drops her there. She lies there. He lies next to her. After a while:

ELIAS

(quietly)
Maybe this is just what it's like.
Maybe this is just what it feels like.

JENNY

What what feels like.

ELIAS

True love.

Jenny is very still. After a while:

ELIAS

Once upon a time . . .
Once upon a time
Once upon a time
There was a statue
standing in the middle of a town square.
It was a statue of a woman.
It was a statue of a woman but no one knew who the woman was.
It had been erected . . .
It had been erected
Hundreds of years before
And none of the townspeople could figure out who she was.
All they knew was that it was a statue a very old statue of a beautiful young woman carrying a bowl of . . .

Apples.

And she stood in the middle of the square and birds sat on her head.

And of course no one knew her name or who had made her but they all called her . . .

Jay—

Julia.

Pause. Jenny and Elias are absolutely still, lying on the couch.

ELIAS

And there was a young man.

And he had grown up in the town and his parents were shepherds and he had grown up among the sheep and goats. Out in the field.

And when he was a little boy his mother took him into town to . . . deposit . . . a check . . . at the bank and on their way there they passed by the statue, by Julia, and the boy fell in love with her.

Who is that, he kept asking his mother.

And the mom didn't know.

Pause.

ELIAS

And the boy grew up and he kept loving the statue and stopping by it every time he came into town to go to the bank or the . . . he would stop by Julia and sometimes he would even leave flowers at her feet.

And other women were interested in him . . . there was a neighbor, a shepherd*ess*—

Jenny giggles.

ELIAS

. . . and she was extremely interested in the boy but he paid her no heed! He only loved the statue. And he grew older

135

and his parents died and he became a shepherd himself and he was happy, in a way. He tended to his flock and at night he made a little fire and read thick books by the light of the fire and once a week, every Sunday after church, he would stop by Julia and talk to her and admire her, uh . . . her uh marble flesh.

And then one Sunday night . . . one Sunday in mid-winter . . . during a particularly harsh snowstorm . . . oh yeah there'd been a particularly harsh snowstorm and so he hadn't been to stop by his beloved statue to say hello. He'd had to stay home and make a fire and put the sheep in the barn and pickle some radishes for the rough winter ahead.

And he was sitting in his little chair by the fire . . .

Jenny's phone dings in her pocket. Elias stops for a split second but then ignores this.

ELIAS

. . . he was sitting in his little chair by the fire and he heard a noise outside his . . .

The phone dings again.

JENNY

Just ignore it.
Sorry.
I thought I turned the sound off.

ELIAS

. . . and he was sitting in his chair and he heard a noise outside the window.
He heard a noise and it sounded like a . . . wail.
It sounded like a woman wailing.
But it was hard to tell because the snow was hitting the glass pane and the wind was howling but every time he thought he was imagining it there it was again, the—

The phone dings again.

ELIAS

—the sound of this woman crying and maybe saying something, he couldn't make out the—

The phone dings again. And then dings again.

JENNY

Sorry.
I love this story.
I'm in love with this story.

ELIAS

Don't you want to see who texted you?

JENNY

No. I want to listen to the rest of the story.

Pause.

ELIAS

Just look to see who texted you.

Jenny tries to roll over and reach into her pocket while he is on top of her. It's kind of awkward. She reaches into the wrong pocket first. Then she starts to reach around again. It becomes clear Elias has to get off of her. He sits up. She sits up. She takes her phone out of her pocket and looks at it.

JENNY

. . . my sister.

She starts to put it back in her pocket.

ELIAS

What'd she say?

JENNY

I didn't look.

ELIAS

Why don't you look to see what she said?

JENNY

Because I can do that later.
I want to hear the rest of the story.

ELIAS

The rest of the story doesn't exist yet.

JENNY

I know. But I want you to / keep—

ELIAS

Just tell me what your sister said. I'll be distracted otherwise.

Jenny sighs and unlocks her phone with her index finger. She clicks on a couple of things.
She reads the texts, holding the phone close to her face.

ELIAS

What'd she say?

Jenny sighs again.

JENNY

She's . . .
She's excited because she . . . she's one of the finalists for this lottery thing in Columbus. It's this stupid lottery that happens once a year and if you win you get a house. And she's been texting me about it because she's a finalist and she's really excited because if you're one of the twenty finalists you get a set of keys to this house . . . it's called the Dream House . . . and everyone shows up with their set of keys but only one of the

finalists have the set of keys that actually opens the front door.
And if you have those keys you win the house. It's so dumb.
She's not going to win.

ELIAS

So what'd she say in the texts?

JENNY

Just that she's excited.
And that it's happening tomorrow.
And that she hopes we're having a good time in Gettysburg.

ELIAS

(still casual, friendly)
Can I see?

JENNY

What.

ELIAS

Can I see her texts?

JENNY

Why?

ELIAS

I'm curious.

JENNY

. . . No.

ELIAS

Why not?

JENNY

Because I just told you what she said.
And I want to hear the rest of the story.

Silence. They are looking at each other. Genevieve is listening, hidden in the shadows.

ELIAS

I wanna read the texts.

JENNY

That's so invasive. No.

Pause.

JENNY

That's not . . .

Jenny puts her phone back in her pocket.

JENNY

I love you.
Please go back to the wailing outside the window.

ELIAS

Were they really from your sister?

JENNY

Yes!

ELIAS

If you're . . .
I really feel like after everything that's happened . . . if you're lying to me again I don't know what to do.

JENNY

Oh my god Eli! I'm not lying to you!
What is happening right now?

ELIAS

If you just show me the texts—

JENNY

I'm sorry, I don't want to be in the kind of relationship where
I have to show my boyfriend my texts because he doesn't trust
me!

ELIAS

You won't ever have to show me any texts again.
Just this one time.
I'll never ask again.

Pause.

ELIAS

I need to know that you were just telling me the truth.
Just now.
And then I'll never ask again.

Pause.

JENNY

No. This is fucked up.
No.
I feel too weird about it.

ELIAS

Because you were lying to me.

JENNY

Because this isn't good.
This isn't good for us.

ELIAS

Give me your phone, Jenny.

JENNY

Oh my god.

He stands.

ELIAS

Give it to me.

JENNY

No!! You're scaring me.

*Elias walks up the stairs and up to the landing. He grabs Saman-
tha. He thrusts her into the air, holding her by the waist.*

ELIAS

Give me your phone.

JENNY

Put her down.

*Elias takes Samantha by the hair, holds it in his fist, and lets her
dangle in the air.*

JENNY

Stop! That's not funny.

ELIAS

Just give me your phone and I'll put her down.

JENNY

No!!! Oh my god this is crazy!!

*Elias slowly lifts up Samantha's skirt with his other hand and pulls
down her underwear.*

JENNY

Eli, stop!

*Samantha's white underwear rests around her ankles. Elias lifts up
her petticoat and inspects Samantha's ass, then her crotch.*

ELIAS

Interesting.
She doesn't have much going on.

Jenny is crying. She covers her face with her hands so she can't see.

ELIAS

Jenny, if you don't give me your phone right now I'm going to lick Samantha's asshole.

Jenny crumples into a ball on the couch, sobbing. Elias, disappointed that she's no longer watching, half-heartedly touches his tongue to Samantha's butt. Then:

ELIAS

. . . I did it.

Jenny is hyperventilating on the couch, her face averted.

ELIAS

Let me see your phone.

She won't look. He watches her.

ELIAS

No?

No response.

ELIAS

Okay.
I'm going to set her on fire.

Jenny bolts upright. Elias walks down the stairs, holding Samantha.

ELIAS

I'm going to melt her face off.

JENNY

That isn't funny.
That's Mertis's doll.

ELIAS

I'll say it was an accident.

He walks over to a candle.

ELIAS

Are you ready?

JENNY

You wouldn't do that.

ELIAS

I will.
I swear to god.
I'll burn her fucking face off if you don't let me see your phone
in five . . . four . . . three . . .

*As he's doing this he's bringing Samantha's head closer and closer
to the flame.*

ELIAS

two . . .

*Jenny, at top volume, starts screaming bloody murder.
It startles him.*

ELIAS

one . . .

*Still screaming, Jenny takes out her iPhone and throws it at him. It
hits him in the chest, then lands on the ground.*

ELIAS

Ow.

Jenny stops screaming, runs over, grabs Samantha, and then runs upstairs.
We hear her footsteps, then the sound of a door slamming. Elias stands there, alone.
After a while Jenny walks back down and stands on the landing. Calmly:

JENNY

I never want to see you again.

Pause.

JENNY

It's over.
Are you listening to me?

And she goes back upstairs. Elias stares at the phone at his feet. The French doors fly open. Mertis sticks her head out.

MERTIS

Is everything all right?

ELIAS

Yeah.
Sorry.

MERTIS

I heard screaming!

ELIAS

Yeah. I'm really sorry.
We're gonna take off in a few minutes.

MERTIS

Why is it so dark out here?

ELIAS

I don't know.

Mertis comes out and switches on a lamp.

MERTIS

Is Genevieve still here?
Or did she go home?

From the corner:

GENEVIEVE

I'm here.

Elias whirls around.

ELIAS

Jesus Christ.

MERTIS

Genevieve! What are you still doing there? Did Joey not come
by to pick you up?

Genevieve doesn't answer.

MERTIS

Oh dear.

Mertis walks around switching on all the lamps.

MERTIS

I don't know who turned all these lights off.

GENEVIEVE

I didn't notice.

MERTIS

Well of course you didn't notice dear Genevieve but that
doesn't mean we want you sitting in the dark.

*Mertis keeps switching on the lamps. There are a lot of them. Elias
bends down and picks up Jenny's phone. He looks at it and presses
the home screen button.*

ELIAS

Locked.

MERTIS

(turning on a lamp)
Excuse me?

ELIAS

It went to sleep and now it's locked.

Mertis gathers a shawl from the back of the couch and throws it around Genevieve's shoulders.

MERTIS

I'm so sorry I left you alone, dearest Genevieve.

GENEVIEVE

How's George?

MERTIS

Oh, worse and worse.

GENEVIEVE

That's too bad.

Pause.

MERTIS

Who wants some Vienna Fingers?

Genevieve nods.

MERTIS

Elias?

Elias nods too. Mertis exits through the French doors. Elias is alone with Genevieve.
He looks at her.

ELIAS

Why didn't you say anything?

Genevieve doesn't answer.

ELIAS

I've never done anything like that before.
FYI.

No answer.

ELIAS

Maybe I'm losing my mind.

Mertis wanders in with the Vienna Fingers on a plate.

MERTIS

Let's all sit together.

She guides Genevieve over to one of tables. Elias gets up, puts Jenny's phone in his pocket, and sits down at the table with them.
Then Mertis suddenly puts a hand to her heart.

MERTIS

Oh my goodness.
I nearly forgot.

GENEVIEVE

Forgot what?

MERTIS

It's the first weekend after Thanksgiving!
I have to light the angel chimes!
No wonder things have been a little strange around here.

Mertis finds the Swedish angel chimes inside a cupboard or a special door, and puts them in the center of the table. She finds some candles and lights them. The angels begin to fly around in circles and chime. It's pretty magical.

MERTIS

There.
Isn't that nice and cozy.

Elias and Genevieve begin munching on Vienna Fingers. Mertis watches them, living vicariously through their munching. After a while:

MERTIS

It's supposed to snow tonight.
Maybe you should spend the night, Genevieve.

ELIAS

We're leaving. So you can have our room.

MERTIS

Oh dear. I'm not sure if you should drive back to New York in a snowstorm.

ELIAS

We'll be fine.
  (to Genevieve)
You can have the Chamberlain room.

GENEVIEVE

  (a little coldly)
I like the Jennie Wade room.

ELIAS

The Jennie Wade room?
Is that on the website?

MERTIS

No, that one's not on the website.

ELIAS

Is it upstairs?

MERTIS

Yes.

ELIAS

I thought it was just the Lincoln and the Jackson and the Chamberlain.

MERTIS

This is just a little extra room that we don't rent out to guests.

ELIAS

But where is it?

MERTIS

Oh, it's right . . . it's attached to the Jackson through a little . . . it's right behind the Jackson. You wouldn't notice it ordinarily.

Pause.

MERTIS

Where's Jenny?

ELIAS

Upstairs.
Packing.

Silence for a while.

MERTIS

(to Elias and Genevieve)
The two of you are being very quiet.

Elias bends over and rubs his temples.

MERTIS

What was that?

ELIAS

Oh. Uh. I'm trying to go off this medication. And I'm . . . every once in a while I get this like . . . these brain zaps. It feels like I'm getting electrocuted or something.

MERTIS

Medication / like—

ELIAS

Uh . . . .
Antidepressants.

MERTIS

I used to be depressed!
Do they help?

ELIAS

Yeah. They've helped a lot. I think. I don't know. Or maybe they've ruined my life. It's hard to tell. Like maybe if I had never been on them I would be crazy now. Like I would be living in a gutter. Or maybe I'd be a world-famous drummer. I have no idea.

The three of them sit in silence and watch the angels fly in circles. Elias reaches forward and runs his finger in and out of the candle flame. After a while:

MERTIS

I had a dream last night that I was standing outside in the snow. Outside of this house looking in. And it was cold and all the lights were on but no one would answer the door.

Pause.

MERTIS

I guess you could call that dream a nightmare.

Pause.

ELIAS

Do either of you know any good scary stories?

Genevieve raises her finger.

GENEVIEVE

There it is.

ELIAS

There what is?

GENEVIEVE

The sound.

ELIAS

What sound?

MERTIS

Genevieve is / convinced—

GENEVIEVE

Shhh.

They all sit and listen to the existence or nonexistence of the sound. Maybe the very very faint sound of the wind howling, barely audible.

MERTIS

I don't like scary stories very much.
I prefer romantic comedies.

GENEVIEVE

Pssh.

MERTIS

Oh, Genevieve. You know there's nothing better than a good romantic comedy.

Pause.

ELIAS

How did you and George meet?

MERTIS

Oh my. That's a long boring story that Genevieve has heard many times before.
    (short pause, to Elias)
The short version is that we wrote each other letters for two years. And then the day we met we got our marriage license. I remember him walking towards me in the Baltimore airport. I'd never met him before and I'd never even seen his picture.

ELIAS

Did he look like you expected?

MERTIS

He looked the same and he looked different.
I imagined it was what it would be like if you cut me open and showed me my heart or liver for the first time.

ELIAS

Is he gonna be okay?
I mean, is he gonna get better?

MERTIS

I don't know, Elias.
I honestly don't know.

Pause.

MERTIS

I will say that meeting him was like walking out of a dark wood. He's not perfect and I'm not perfect and we have our hard times but I remember moving towards him through Terminal 4 and it was like emerging from the cold and into the sun.

Like waking up from the bad dream that was my life before him.

And all the confusion and fear and self-hatred that I'd always felt in the presence of other people . . .

I was shedding it like a skin.

The spell had ended.

And I remember thinking: everything is possible.

If this is possible, anything is possible.

After a while:

MERTIS

Let's listen to some music.

Mertis gets up and walks over to the little jukebox. She puts in a new CD and carefully forwards to a track: "Les oiseaux dans la charmille" from Tales of Hoffmann starts playing. Contented, Mertis comes back the table.
The three of them sit and listen to the song and watch the angels fly around in circles.
About halfway through it Jenny's phone dings inside Elias's pocket.
Elias takes it out and puts it on the table in front of him.
Mertis leans over and peers curiously at the phone.

MERTIS

Who's John?

END OF PLAY

ANNIE BAKER grew up in Amherst, Massachusetts. Her other full-length plays include *The Flick* (Pulitzer Prize for Drama, Hull-Warriner Award, Susan Smith Blackburn Prize, Obie Award for Playwriting), *Circle Mirror Transformation* (Obie Award for Best New American Play, Drama Desk nomination or Outstanding Play), The Aliens (Obie Award for Best New American Play), *Body Awareness* (Drama Desk nomination for Outstanding Play, John Gassner Award nomination) and an adaptation of Chekhov's *Uncle Vanya* (Drama Desk nomination for Outstanding Revival), for which she also designed the costumes. Her plays have been produced at more than two hundred theaters throughout the U.S. and in more than a dozen countries. Recent honors include a Guggenheim Fellowship, the Steinberg Playwright Award, an American Academy of Arts and Letters Award, and the 2015–16 Cullman Fellowship at the New York Public Library. She is a resident playwright at Signature Theatre.